LOST BUT NOT FORGOTTEN

The Story of
Albert (Bert) Henri Menere
No. 7283

A soldier of the 35th Battalion AIF

BRANDT WARD

Lost But Not Forgotten
The Story of Albert (Bert) Henri Menere: A
Soldier of the 35th Battalion AIF

First published in Australia by Brandt Ward 2025

A catalogue record for this
book is available from the
National Library of Australia

ISBN: 978-0-646-72418-8

Book cover image: The Everett Collection © (Shutterstock 785840674)

Typesetting and design by Publicious Book Publishing
Published in collaboration with Publicious Book Publishing
www.publicious.com.au

Albert Henri Menere, 7283

AIF 3rd Division, 9th Infantry Brigade, 35th Battalion

Born: 11th March 1880. Hopedale Farm, Coreen, NSW.
Profession: Engineer.
Married: 9th September 1907.
Wife: Blanche Adeline Menere nee: Grass.
Died: 2nd October 1917. Zonnebeke, Belgium.
Father: George Edward Menere.
Mother: Elizabeth Anne Evans.
Children: Aubrey, Raymond, Aureole, Albert, Edward, Leila

Grandfather's Chair

By Brandt, 2006.

In the corner, in his old chair,
He sits with memories, beyond compare.
Easier to sit than to stand,
A life well-lived, with love at hand.

Old and frail, his time draws near,
But this little girl brings him cheer.
She plays at his feet, without a care,
Her laughter fills the twilight air.

She smiles and captures her Pa's heart,
Unaware of life's impending depart.
He looks at her with love so deep,
His legacy in her eyes, he'll keep.

In his favourite chair, he sits and sighs,
A lifetime of love, no goodbyes.
His eyes may dim, but love shines bright,
For this little girl, his heart's delight.

He wishes her well, in silent lament,
Knowing his time is nearly spent.
She looks up with innocence and trust,
His life's purpose, in her he must.

This book is for June, his never-knew,
A testament to love, forever true.

For June,
Who never knew her Grandfather.

Forward

In *Lost But Not Forgotten*, Brandt Ward invites us on a deeply personal and profoundly moving journey into the life of Albert Henri Menere—his great-grandfather whose wartime legacy had long remained obscured by silence and time. Through meticulous research and evocative storytelling, Ward unearths a narrative that is both intimate and historically resonant, shedding light on a man whose brief but poignant service on the Western Front ended in tragedy.

Albert's story is not one of battlefield glory, but of quiet courage and heartbreaking misfortune. Killed in action shortly after arriving at the front, his fate stands as a stark reminder of the countless lives altered or extinguished by the randomness of war. Ward's account does more than reconstruct Albert's final days; it restores his place in the family's memory and in the broader tapestry of Australian history.

What makes this book especially compelling is its ability to weave colourful anecdotes and historical detail into a portrait of a time when the world was irrevocably changed. Ward captures the long shadow cast by World War One over Australian society, its impact on families, communities, and national identity. In doing so, he not only honours Albert's legacy but also gives voice to a generation whose stories are too often lost to history.

Lost But Not Forgotten is a testament to the power of remembrance. It reminds us that even the briefest lives can leave enduring marks, and that through the act of uncovering and sharing these stories, we keep their memory alive.

Colonel (Retd) Brian Bailey CSC
2025

Contents

Introduction

Over 60,000 Australians died on the battlefields of World War 1. None were buried on their home soil except for one, the Unknown Soldier interred at the Australian War Memorial in 1993. Their names exist in shrines throughout the country in parks, memorial gardens, and on the walls of the local RSL clubs. The Australian War Memorial in Canberra has their names carved in stone, but they were buried where they died, in the war cemeteries of France, Belgium, Egypt, Gallipoli, Greece and Crete. Approximately a third of the dead have no known graves. Unable to be identified or obliterated by high explosives, their remains are as scattered as the haunting memories of their loved ones left behind. It has been over a century since WW1 and as the generations have passed, so have the memories of so many Australian soldiers. Theirs is almost a lost generation.

Albert Henri Menere, my great grandfather, was one of the soldiers killed and lost. During 1917 he was killed in Belgium, buried the same evening, and never seen whole again. The most tangible connection between the man and his AIF service is a name on a wall in Ypres, France. His legacy exists in his descendants living free in our amazing country. This book happened by chance. An afternoon with a dying woman and the pointing of her finger. This was the spark that ignited a decade's journey in resurrecting the memory of a family member. This is how the afternoon unfolded:

June Ward (nee Lowe), my mother, was in the final months of life. At home on the Gold Coast, she was bedridden. Most afternoons after work, I visited her and spent an hour or so chatting before going home to my own family. The conversations were usually light and happy. Her demeanour in no way reflected her approaching date with destiny. On this particular afternoon, she pointed to a chest of drawers and asked me to get something out, probably her purse. "*Not that draw, the bottom one,*" she indicated. June was reliant upon oxygen at the time and her mobility was just about non-existent. So, I bent down to get her purse and then, to the side, I spotted a piece of embroided fabric. It had an Australian Coat of Arms, a studio photograph of a soldier, and a message '*To my Dear Wife*' sewn onto it. It was a cushion cover.[1] Hence, the inquisition began: "What is this, who is this, when and why ?"

I was 49 years old at the time, and this was the first time he had ever been mentioned. My mother's grandfather had never been discussed. Like many Australian households, I just don't think it was of interest. Perhaps because too many generations had passed? My mother told me that the man in the photo was Albert Menere. Thus, an insatiable interest in this man and his story began. I decided I was going to resurrect Albert's memory from the dust and mud of Belgium by telling his story the best I could. There wasn't much to work with. No other photographs existed, no medals, no letters, no first-hand accounts of the man existed on my mother's side of the family. Internet research revealed very little information about family connections and generations past.

A few years later in 2012, I went on a pilgrimage of sorts to find where he fell. This took me to Belgium and Polygon Wood for that year's ANZAC Day ceremony officiated by Brendon Nelson, who was then Australia's Ambassador to Belgium, NATO and the EU. From Polygon Wood I headed to Zonnebeke 2km to the east, almost walking distance. This is the town where Albert Menere was killed. My early research indicated he was buried 150 yards (130m) from the parapet adjacent to the railway station. I found the spot, raised beer, had a drink and thanked Bert.

His death on the battlefield left a widow and six young children. His wife, Blanche Menere, my Great Grandmother, remarried in 1926 to William Ogg.

I tried to tell the story within the historical and social context of the times, particularly 1917. I read many articles written by those who experienced the war, mothers and fathers at home, soldiers on the front. Their stories gave me an insight into the mindset of the time. I hope that my account of their thoughts and emotions ring true.

This work is a mixture of fact and fiction. The people, places, dates and events in Albert Menere's story are true and as accurate as my research could ascertain. The relationships between Albert Menere and the other people in his story were developed under an umbrella of creative licence. The soldiers are real; their positions

---

[1] See appendix 1.

in the AIF accurate and the time-lines true. The footnotes are extensive with the intention to give immediate in-depth relevance to what is happening on that page of Albert Menere's story. Hopefully, Albert Menere's name will be spoken aloud, again.

Brandt Ward, MEd. (Leadership and Management)
June 2025

Chapter 1

Happy times at the Town and Country Hotel.

Here's to the four hinges of Friendship -
Swearing, Lying, Stealing and Drinking.
When you swear, swear by your country.
When you lie, lie for a pretty woman,
When you steal, steal away from bad company
And when you drink, drink with me.

'Friendship'[2], author unknown.

The public bar at the Town and Country wasn't as happy as it used to be. Albert (Bert) Menere drank there a lot, but not as often as the younger lads of the area. The likes of Percy (Spider) Dwyer, Walter (Walt) Moore, Richard, and the brewery mob would drink there every afternoon from knock off till closing. Thanks to the ruckus caused by the army recruits at Liverpool on the 14th of February 1916, the NSW Government legislated a 6.00pm closing for all pubs.[3] So, the boys' time to get their fill of beer was substantially shortened. Once a week, perhaps twice, Bert would sit in the western corner overlooking Unwin's Bridge Road, listening to the stories these young blokes would spin. With a middy[4] of Resches in hand, Bert would listen to their hometown yarns about the local girls, football and almost anything else that took the fancy

---

[2] Simplepoetry.com., retrieved 10.5.25.
[3] On February 14, 1916, the 'Liverpool Riot' occurred when Australian Imperial Force (AIF) recruits from the Liverpool training camp in Sydney rioted and caused widespread damage. This event led to the introduction of 6:00 pm hotel closing hours in New South Wales, Victoria, and Tasmania.
[4] Colloquial term for half-pint of beer predominantly used in NSW and WA.

for these hard-working blokes. Even though they were all mates, Bert preferred to just listen.

Bert often rejected their attempts to draw him into their fray at the bar. "Hey Bert, come over here, away from the window with all your mates, Bert sitting alone, and tell Johnno 'ere what you did to that apprentice back in Corowa the day he ate your lunch". Bert felt that they considered him to be somewhat wiser and older, being thirty-six years and all. None the less, their vision of Bert, all of 5'5", wrapping a chain around the waist of 'Donger' Mick and then welding it to the metal workbench always sparked yells of approval. "Took 'em till teatime to get him out and nearly cost me my job". "Shit it was funny" he would think to himself as he smiled and slowly shook his head. "He never ate my lunch again!"

His neighbor from King St was Dessey Lowe[5] and like Bert, he enjoyed a beer. They always had something to talk about and felt comfortable in each other's company. Both being blessed with the responsibilities of fatherhood may have been their common ground. Des's son Hugh, being of voting age, was older than any of Bert's brood of six. Des was also a Newtown Football Club supporter, and this was undoubtedly his area of expertise which only the bravest would dare debate. To criticize the Jets'[6] weekend performance in any form or matter might incur a ferocious verbal attack from Des. He loved his footy! And, if a Jet's loss coincided with half a dozen Saturday afternoon schooners, stand back because the fists might fly. No one really cared because Des couldn't fight very well and wasn't much bigger than Bert. Everyone knew that there would be hell to pay with Hughey if anyone laid a hand on his dad. Any scuffle with Dessey Lowe at the Town and Country Hotel on 'footy day' always ended with a laugh and Des slurring some sort of indignation towards the younger crew indicating something along the lines that things would be a might different if he was thirty years younger. "Why don't the lotta of yous piss off to the ladies' lounge where ya belong?" was one of Des's more frequently used barbs to close the discussion down.

---

[5] Sourced from RMS 'Osterley' manifest. Dessey was father of Hugh Lowe (7274) and A.H.Menere's next door neighbour. The stated address of Des and Hugh Lowe being 58 King St, St Peters (now The Princess Highway).
[6] Newtown Jets being a foundation team in the NSW Rugby League.

During early 1915 Spider Dwyer and Walt came rushing into the front bar bragging about a great fish they had just landed out of the Cook's River down off the Bay. "Have a go at me hands Bert!" Walt barked with a touch of confidence knowing that the story was going to be a good one. "Cut to pieces because of that bastard Jew fish that's now sittin' out the back on Spider's Dray.[7] I fought him for twenty minutes with only a hand line".

Heads were beginning to turn and in no time the two had secured the attention of the entire pub. Even a few of the local girls had wandered around from the Ladies' Lounge to see what the commotion was. With a captivated audience of about twenty, and with great glee, the story was retold again by Spider for the benefit of the new listeners; the language now being less colourful due to the presence of the female folk. "Must be a fair dinkum 50lbs" Spider said spreading his freckled, red-haired, long lanky arms as far wide as possible. "Walt was in two minds to hitch the bloody line to the horse and drag the bastard out, but I convinced him that the oysters on the rocks would likely snap the line". Having said this, Spider seemed to lay part claim on the prize fish which was, in a very short time hence, to become the talking piece amongst the pub's patrons for the longest time.

"Show us the fish you cocky bastards" was the sentiment from the mob and with that Spider and Walt led the entire front bar contingent out the back where the prize lay. As they stepped between the two tables that made up the beer garden, both had smiles on them like they had just picked the winner in the last at Randwick. Suddenly, heads spun in response to Walt screaming at Spider to pass him the horse whip so he could "belt the shit out of those 'efin' dogs".

With tears of laughter, the last the mob saw of Spider and Walt on that Saturday afternoon was the two of them running down Campbell Street chasing the local dogs who had, with great stealth, thieved the prize fish straight from the dray. By the time the thieving canines were apprehended very little of the fish remained and what was left had been keenly marinated in road-side grime and manure. Still one of the funniest things Bert and the front bar crew had ever been witness to.

---

[7] An early Australian expression for a horse-drawn, two-wheeled cart without sides.

Spider[8] and Walt Moore[9] were killed in action eighteen months later at Pozieres in France. They were both Newtown boys and they died on the same day.[10] They fished, drank, fought, and died together. They were mates.

---

[8] Percy Mingo Dwyer, 1st Battalion, 2980, KIA France 22.7.16.
[9] Walter Moore, 1st Battalion, 3410, KIA France 22.7.16.
[10] AWM, 1st Battalion, Roll of Honour.

Chapter 2
At home with Blanche.

At home I feel the warm embrace,
Of family and wife, secure and safe.
How can I stay in this safe cocoon,
Knowing others are dying, in the wet and the gloom?

'Torn', by Brandt, 2025

The Christmas of 1916 was hard. The drought persisted back home in Corowa and the brothers were always complaining about the difficulties on the land.[11] Bert could not give them the sympathy that had been extended to them in the past by their city dwelling relatives. Bert's heart was heavy, his mind fogged and tormented by the memories and mental wounds created by Spider's and Walt's deaths in France. How did they die? A bullet, an explosion or heaven forbid a bayonet from Fritz. Deep down Bert knew that a bayonet into the belly would be the worst. "Would I be brave enough to front the enemy at such close range? I'm only small. How would I go confronting the likes of a bigger man, charging full stride with rifle and bayonet extended? Would I be brave?" All these questions tested his mental resolve. "Maybe I should have responded earlier to Billy Hughes's call to arms."[12] That Christmas was the worst.

Bert's beloved Blanche knew that her husband was troubled. As Bert regularly perused the *Daily Telegraph* newspaper looking through the names of the latest AIF casualties, grieving over the

---

[11] Albert Menere moved to Sydney sometime after 1912, Aureole (the author's grandmother) being born in Corowa in 1912.
[12] A letter sent by prime Minister William M (Billy) Hughes and dated 15th December 1915, was sent to all eligible men.

unthinkable numbers of those young men who would never return, Blanche consoled him. Her consoling was never with words. Just her look and a touch were enough to bring his focus back to what really counted in his world, the children.

True to the ideals of an Irish Catholic, the six children were embraced by the love and devotion of Albert and Blanche Menere. As a family they lived by the laws of the Catholic Church and after 10 years of marriage the love and respect had sometimes been strained but never extinguished.[13] Aubrey, Raymond, Aureole[14], Albert (junior), Edward and Leila were all part of the family. It was considered, without question or reason, they would always be together. Things, however, were about to change.

It was a morning newspaper article sometime around Christmas 1916 that changed it all for Bert. The celebration of the Holy Birth was marred by the headlines *Stalemate in the trenches makes for a bleak mid-winter*.[15] In short, Christmas morning readers were confronted with this:

> *"Dec.25 The third Christmas of the war has been the bleakest yet. Two years ago, the men of Europe had gone to war cheerily confident of being home by Christmas. Today there is no such optimism. Neither side achieved the great breakthrough they sought in 1916 – and the cost in lives was immense.*
>
> *At Verdun unofficial estimates of losses are 700,000 men. Further west, the great British offensive at the Somme proved even bloodier: 650,000 Allied soldiers perished, most of them British along with 500,000 Germans. In places the frontlines were only changed by a mile or two, but rarely for long…"*

Bert reflected, "In 1899 I was twenty when the call to arms was heard. Going to South Africa and fighting so the English could have access to diamonds, 'natural resources' as the papers referred

---

[13] Albert Henri Menere married Blanche Adelaide Grass in 1906, in New South Wales.
[14] Aureole Evelyn Menere is the author's grandmother and June Elaine Ward's (nee Lowe) mother. June is the author's mother.
[15] 'The stalemate in the trenches makes for a bleak mid-winter…', Chronicle of the 20th Century, p221.

to them; well, that was never going to get me in." However, the Western Front, Percy Dwyer, Walter Moore and all the others from 'here and about' that are dead, presented a whole new story and Blanche knew it. For Bert, duty was calling so loud that it was becoming impossible to ignore.

For the next three weeks tension between Bert and Blanche was obvious. Blanche would throw every guilt-laden argument at Bert to change his mind. The children, his work as an engineer[16] and his Church laid foundation to Blanche's arguments that, in her heart, she knew she was not going to win. "Other men need me, Australia needs me, and I need to sacrifice something towards stopping this aggression and the killing." Bert knew with absolute certainty that the guilt that would surely come if he did not become part of this fight would be impossible to deal with. What would he say to his sons if he did not do something and fight?

Australia Day 1917 was a Friday, and it was bloody hot. Dessey Lowe called to Bert from over the back fence at about 9.30am. Bert thought he was arranging an afternoon beer. He was wrong. "Hughey is going to enlist tomorrow, what am I gonna do?" he said in a voice quiet yet controlled. They both knew that nothing could be done and that there was a chance that tomorrow, enlistment day, Des Lowe may be hugging his son for the last time. Des and Bert did have that beer on Australia Day, 1917 and they spoke of family, mates, politics and the future. For the first time in memory, footy did not get a mention. Who was to know that this was one of the last times Bert would have a beer with his good friend and neighbor?

After dinner that evening, Bert told Blanche that he was enlisting the next morning. She cried yet never raised her voice. Her demeanor that evening was one of acceptance and sorrow. Her consoling look and touch, that so soothed him in the past, was not there. Blanche needed Bert's love; the children needed their father. Blanche knew that the consequences for a widow bringing up six children alone would be dire. Bert knew that the consequences of growing old without helping the war effort would be no less.

---

[16] Engineer being listed as occupation on enlistment form.

Chapter 3

Enlistment Day Saturday 27th January 1917: 15 days before embarkation.

The nations take their places
Upon the board of Fate,
With stern, determined faces
And spirits hot with hate.
The battle-drums are rattling,
War's shining blades are bared ;
My countrymen ! cease prattling —
Get ready ! Be prepared!

Extract from 'To Australians', by Arthur Bayldon[17]

Before the war, Saturday mornings always held a sort of 'sacredness' for the family. Not in the same way as their Sunday Mass, but in the way that it was the start of the weekend. A couple of days off and it always felt good. Blanche would walk to the newsagent, always with little Aureole, and sometimes with any of the other children that were in a mind to go. Not Aubrey or Raymond, however, being boys, they were long gone, probably fishing, or exploring the bush down the road near Tempe with the other boys of the neighborhood. She'd return with the Saturday Morning Herald, then with a cup of tea and toast, Bert's weekend would begin. News from abroad, classifieds, the comics and the form guide would occupy for a duration measured by two cups of tea, maybe three. Nowadays the Saturday Morning Herald, and come to think of it Saturday mornings, no longer felt the same.

---

[17] Arthur Bayldon, 'To Australians', 1905, Sourced Australianculture.org, 10.5.25.

Just another day of newspaper information about names, numbers, who's dead, who's maimed, what's rationed, troops, the Hun – an overload that would continue to cast one into yet another week void of colour and promise, just guilt and sorrow.

Saturday 17 January, Blanch may have gone to the newsagents, Bert will never know. Together with Hughey Lowe, he left at 7.30am for the short walk to the enlistment station up the road. As was the norm for the past few years, the last Saturday of each month the doors of the St Peter's Masonic Lodge Hall were opened to new prospects to the Australian Imperial Force (AIF). As Bert walked through the single wooded door his emotions ran rampant. "Finally, I can live with myself – I'm doing my part". He felt guilty and torn between risking the sanctity and security of his family and serving his country. He was nervous. His inevitable place on the right-hand side of God may be realized sooner than later. As with most Catholics, Bert viewed death as a change rather than an ending. Hughey on the other hand, well he seemed bloody excited.

Form after form needed to be filled out. There must have been at least 30 blokes signing on the day and the wait was drawn out. Thirty enlistees, three tables and a dozen chairs for sitting in. "I hope they run the war better than they're running this bloody circus" Hughey said to Bert loud enough to invoke a laugh from those around him and a 'stink-eye' death stare from the army's administration crew.

The first form Bert filled out was an 'Application to enlist in the Australian Imperial Force' and with his signature he did declare the following:

> I, ALBERT HENRI MENERE, hereby offer myself for Enlistment in the Australian Imperial Force for Active Service Abroad, and undertake to enlist in the manner described, if I am accepted by the Military Authorities, within one month of date hereof.[18]

And furthermore, Bert did take the following oath:

> I, ALBERT HENRI MENERE, swear that I will well and truly serve our Sovereign Lord the King in the Australian Imperial Forces from 27 January, 1917 until the end of the

---

[18] Taken from A.H.Menere's Application to Enlist in A.I.F form dated 27.01.17, p1.

war, and a further period of four months thereafter unless sooner lawfully discharged or removed there from; and that I will resist His Majesty's enemies and cause His Majesty's peace to be kept maintained; and that I will in all matters to my service, faithfully discharge my duty accordingly. SO HELP ME GOD[19]

Unbeknown to Bert at the time it was this signature that would seal his fate as a fallen ANZAC on the Belgium front in eight months' time. At 11.30am it was announced to all concerned that they were to report to Victoria Barracks, temporarily situated at the Sydney Show Grounds, Monday morning for the medical examination.[20] The final piece of paperwork Hughey and Bert were fronted with on that day was the A.I.F Attestation paper.

Hughey was a bit confused with the difference between this form and the other enlistment form he had just filled out earlier. Bert explained that it was just a way of them knowing who exactly you are and that you are not a fleeing criminal or something. Hughey had a bit of a whinge but reacted appropriately when the recruiting corporal barked "the only way your 'gonna' get paid your 10 shillings a day[21] was by signing ya bloody signature, so get on with it so I can get out of here and down to the pub for my lunch". The mention of pay certainly got Hughey jumping. He also let go with some comment about the corporal's assertive demeanor (said just soft enough for the somewhat large corporal to hear but not understand). The recruiting corporal was a scary but solemn looking bloke with his left arm missing from the elbow. Bert's thoughts led him to wonder how he lost his arm, and where he was when it happened.

In short, Bert and Hughey had to furnish the following information on the Attestation Papers before getting out of the Masonic Hall and back home for their last days before training and deployment. For Bert, his read as follows:

---

[19] Taken from A.H.Menere's Application to Enlist in A.I.F form dated 27.01.17, p2.
[20] Taken from A.H. Menere's Medical History Form dated 29.01.17.
[21] Being the nominal pay rate as noted on point 14 of all A.I.F Attestation Papers.

Born: Corowa N.S.W
Age: 36 years, 10 months.
Trade: Engineer
Next of Kin: Wife, Blanche Adelaide Edith Menere of
56 King St, St Peters, Sydney, NSW
Rate of pay: Not to exceed 10/- per day.

And as a final attestation Bert did declare the following:

I, ALBERT HENRI MENERE do solemnly declare that the above answers made by me to the above questions (relating to the attestation paper) are true, and I am willing and hereby voluntarily agree to serve in the Military Forces of the Commonwealth of Australia within or beyond the limits of the Commonwealth.[22] And further agree to allot not less than four fifths of the pay payable to me from time to time during my service for the support of my wife and children.

The usual amount retained for the wife and children was two fifths of one's pay; however, Bert knew Blanche's need for the money would be far greater than his, so he adjusted it so four fifths went directly to family.[23] Maybe this would ease the guilt he felt knowing that he was leaving them?

---

[22] Final declaration by A.H. Menere on Attestation Papers signed and dated 27th January 1917.
[23] Signed and notarised on original Attestation Paper.

Chapter 4
The Medical Monday 29th January 1917:
13 Days before embarkation.

It's not long now boys,
Till we wave goodbye.
To our mates, to our wives,
To our kids, and our joys.

We're off to France boys,
To the gloom and the mud.
Hopefully we'll return boys,
To the ones we love.

'Embarkation Day', by Brandt, 2025

The medical examination was to take place next. All up, the trip to the Victoria Barracks at the Sydney Showground took about an hour. Bert sat quietly on the train moving slowly to the rhythmic harmonics of the 3137 steam train. The cigarette butts embedded in the bitumen composite floor of the train grabbed his attention, he didn't understand why. Hughey was nowhere to be seen. He wasn't on the same train as agreed so Bert figured he may have made his way out there on his own. Maybe he missed the whole thing because of the big night his mates put on at the Town and Country pub on the Saturday afternoon? Alas, on arriving at the Barracks, there was Hughey with Des by his side amongst perhaps 1000 other recruits. It was obvious Des was struggling with his boy's impending departure into an unknown and dangerous future. Bert could see in Des's eyes the same strength, yet underlying sadness, expressed by Blanche and the older children. Thank heavens most of his children were too young to realize the gravity of the situation.

Two years earlier there would have been no chance of Albert Henri Menere successfully enlisting. Being small in stature, his 5'4¾" height would have been about two inches shy of making the grade. However, being three years into the bloodiest war in history, the AIF's selection criteria changed somewhat. The Prime Minister, Billy Hughes' failure to secure a national conscription for the second time was compounded by increasing casualties abroad. This needed to be addressed. More soldiers were required and the Mother country's call was loud. Newspapers were pleading for men to enlist. Jingoistic posters calling all eligible men to support their 'Aussie' brothers in Europe were appearing everywhere. They were colourful, patriotic and exuded a notion of adventure. The media were reporting on stories of heroism focusing on Australian characters to convince men to join up out of a sense adventure, pride and perhaps even shame. The propaganda machine jumped on the colourful stories of an English merchant navy deserter called Kirkpatrick.

As a young man Kirkpatrick ended up in Australia working as a coalminer south of Sydney and for some reason took on the name 'Simpson'. Simpson was a first-day lander at Gallipoli and was posted to the 3rd Field Ambulance. His exploits going into 'no-mans', working alone, ignoring orders, and retrieving the wounded with a string of donkeys were the sort of stories the media needed and certainly exploited. This campaign and lowing the height-limit criteria for enlistment contributed to the much-needed influx of new recruits during late 1916 and into 1917. Bert was one of them.

Stated on Bert's medical form (A.M. Form D.I) he exhibited half a dozen scars, was short in stature and a weight of 138lbs. These were deemed 'slight defects, but not sufficient to cause rejection'.[24] He was vaccinated against Cholera, confirmed that he was sane and did not suffer from consumption. Captain C. G. Allen of the Medical Corp signed him off as fit and as of 3.30pm on Wednesday 29 January 1917, Albert Henri Menere was a soldier of the A.I.F.

---

[24] A.H.Menere Medical History, point (b) page 1.

By the end of the day, Bert was exhausted. The final instruction given to him and the rest of the 24th Reinforcements was to report for duty at the First Depot Battalion Camp, Liverpool, 10.00am Wednesday, 7 February 1917.[25] At that stage there was no mention of when they would be leaving the shores of their homeland toward adventure and the unknown.

Earlier, Bert had arranged to meet up with Des and Hughey at the Imperial Hotel in Paddington before returning to St Peters. "Meet you across the road for a quiet one," Hughey shouted as the Medical Corporal led him into the inoculation room. A quiet one! By the time the three of them arrived, Oxford Street was overflowing with what seemed every man, son, horse, brother and mate in the eastern suburbs of Sydney. Everyone loved the 'Imperial' as it was this pub that Mr. Resches himself, Edmund Resches once owned whilst building his brewing empire. There was laughing, yelling and a lot of back-slapping. What a joyous sight it was. In the two hours before six o'clock closing, Bert managed to tuck away half a dozen schooners – far beyond his usual manageable quota of two. Bert was excited to be going. In his heart he knew he was doing the right thing. Looking out over all those young blokes outside and inside the pub, he knew he had to be part of it. He needed to be with them, amongst the fighting, looking after each other. At almost 37 years of age, he was the old rooster amongst a cocky crew of lads. He was where he needed to be.

The rusting wrought iron gate in front of his King Street home squeaked as Bert opened it, giving Blanche fair warning that her husband was home. It wasn't enough time to disguise her crying. Her eyes were red and puffy, her gaze was distant, but her heart was breaking. She said very little; she did not need to.

---

[25] The 7th and the 9th of February are indicated as revaccination dates for A.H.Menere on medial History Form. Signed off by C.G.ALLEN Capt. AMC it can be assumed that this was part of pre-embarkation period at Liverpool Depot, now known as Holsworthy.

Chapter 5

Time to go.

"I stood at the door where he went out,
Full grown man ruddy and stout.
I heard the march of the trampling feet,
Slow and steady come down the street.
And just for a moment as he went by,
I had sight of his face and the flash of his eye."

Extract from 'War', by Mary Gilmore, 1918.

Between enlisting and reporting for duty, Bert had nine days to get things in order. Notifying the blokes at work that he was going off to the war was easy – they understood. His extended family did not share the same acceptance and understanding. They could not understand why he had volunteered to serve. As soon as word got out that he had given his oath to serve King and Country, telegrams from all over the place started to come in. You would think best wishes would be the prevailing sentiment – but not amongst the brothers and in-laws. Why are you going? What about the children? Why would a father of six want to go to war? "You are 36 years old for heaven's sake". Bert has always held little tolerance towards these shallow family attitudes and failed to respond to any request for justification of his decision. Maybe he just did not have an answer? Bert wasn't that close to his family. They worked on the land in the Corowa/Bundalong region of Victoria.

Bert's father died when he was just five, but his mother was alive and remarried Henry Bartlett soon after her first husband's death. She was 18 years old when Bert was born and they remained close even though they were far apart. Correspondence between the two was scant during the short period between enlisting and embarking. As was expected, trepidation and worry lurked in every corner of his mother's mind. A mother's burden on the home front during war is a force hard to harness, no less the burden of the possibility of a mother losing a son.

Blanche quietly and with a reverence of despair, gave Bert her blessing. Their love for each other was undeniable. The meals during that final week were nice. The talks subdued and short. Everything Blanche and Bert did during that final week together seemed to be focused on maintaining calmness. At 7.30am on Wednesday 7 February 1917, it was this calmness that almost overwhelmed him. He stepped out onto the porch of 56 King Street, St Peters for the last time and for that instant in time not a sound could be heard. The traffic of horses and trams along what was normally a busy street seemed to grind to a halt as if to paint a picture of serenity of which Bert could take with him into the trenches. The serenity of the moment was finally broken by the squeak and the clank of the front gate as it closed behind him. "I'll fix it when I get back," Bert thought to himself.

Walk, tram, train were the modes of transport undertaken when travelling from St Peters to Liverpool. The main South Line of the NSW Rail between Newtown and Liverpool took most of the day. Bert didn't get out into the western suburbs often, so the new scenery took his mind off his destination. He enjoyed the bushland as he crossed the Georges River and by the time the train had passed through Lidcombe and Regent's Park it was full of the newest recruits to the AIF. A cup of tea and a sandwich was pretty much in the forefront of Bert's mind so when the train had an extended stop at Cabramatta, he was one of the first off the train for some refreshments. It was a battle, but he got his tea in time to drink it and get back on the train before its departure from the station.

The 1st Depot Battalion Camp at Liverpool was busy, noisy and colourless. No training, no guns, no manuals were given out to any of the newly enlisted. Within one hour of their first parade, it became common knowledge that they were to leave on Saturday. The only things they received over the next three days was a uniform, more inoculations, and talk after talk about army rules and regulations.

Until late 1916, basic training, weapons training and general induction were part of the program delivered at the Liverpool and Casula camps. A change came and it was decided to get the new recruits to the front as soon as possible. Most of the training would wait until Durrington.[26] The time journeying to England was to be utilised with some of the intended induction syllabus being covered in the eight weeks traversing the oceans. The rules and regulations thrown at the new recruits were many and quite often reflected the antiquated mindset of a bygone English army. After the English led fiasco at Fromelles, the AIF started to take control of their own troops by departing from the Napoleonic tactics used by Britain during the previous years of the war. The Australian Command recognized this and adjusted the training of soldiers and the strategies of command. However, an army needs discipline and rules. Many of the Australian soldiers had difficulty understanding this and whether on or off the battlefield, they were inclined to take matters and tactics into their own hands.

George Moore[27] was part of Bert's Company. At 43 he was another old rooster amongst the 'youngins'. George and Bert became friends and would spend time together during the voyage to the Mother Land. Bert sensed that George was a bit of a scoundrel which made him wary, none-the-less they became mates. During one parade in the main quad at the Liverpool camp, an enthusiastic sergeant was explaining army rules regarding leave and the consequences of not adhering to these rules. George whispered to those around him "If the beer is cold and the women warm, I'll risk it!" This attitude stuck with George and would come back and bite him in the near future. They all laughed and were instantly reprimanded by the sergeant who was over 6 feet tall, loud and with a presence that demanded immediate adherence to any instruction. His stare was formidable. "He is one scary bastard!" Bert and George thought to themselves.

Army regulations involved the final preparation to Attestation Papers, rolls, allotments and pay-books. The issuing of clothing and some basic equipment followed in due course. Standing

---

[26] Durrington being one of the main AIF training camps in the Salisbury Plains of England.
[27] George Moore age 43, Regimental Number 7285 embarked on the Osterley with A.H. Menere.

straight and still for roll call, vaccinations and inoculations gradually erased the civilian in Bert opening the new and final chapter in the life of Bert Menere, a soldier of the A.I.F. The three days and two nights spent at Liverpool went quickly. The beds were uncomfortable, the company loud and boisterous, the food adequate. Bert got a glimpse of himself in uniform. He was happy with what he saw.

Chapter 6

Embarkation day, the adventure begins.

Farewell dear Australia, the land of our birth.
Farewell to our loved ones, our home and our heart,
No more the sweet wattle, all laden with gold.
For one (last) glimpse of its beauty, we'd love to behold.

Extract from poem 'A soldier's Farewell', author unknown.

Daybreak on Saturday 10 February 1917 and the journey to England began. The 24th Reinforcements of the 1st Battalion were marched out through the camp's grounds to Liverpool railway station. Their marching had improved considerably since the Thursday just passed as this was the only army skill so far imparted to the men and boys. The three-mile march was a boisterous one. The route was via the Hume Highway then to Macquarie Street (Liverpool) leading to the station. Bert did more listening and thinking than talking. The cheers from the public were reassuring. During that short march he felt solace in the fact that he was doing the right thing. Yes, Australia was truly the lucky country; worth protecting. On arrival at the railway station, the troops then proceeded in three specifically scheduled troop trains to Central Railway Station. The sandwiches and tea supplied at the station set up for a comfortable run into the city. Bert's slouch hat felt good.

Embarkation onto the R.M.S. 'Osterley'[28] took place at Woolloomooloo. The transport, normally a mail cargo ship until

---

[28] The RMS 'Osterley' was a 12,129 gross ton ship, length 535ft x beam 63.2ft, two funnels, two masts, twin screw and a speed of 18 knots. There was accommodation for 280-1st, 130-2nd and 900-3rd class passengers. Built by London & Glasgow Shipbuilding Co, Glasgow for the Orient Steam Nav.Co. She started her maiden voyage on 6th Aug.1909 when she

refitted for troop transport in 1915, anchored in the nearby Rushcutters Bay. Sydney Harbour was a sight to behold. The glassy blueness of the water being split by the bow of the ferry 'Kurrule' making its way to Circular Quay. Salt in the air, gulls in the sky, Bert was readying himself. The next day, Sunday 11 February 1917, whilst still at anchor, the Osterley was surrounded by dozens of small motor launches full of families and general well-wishers. Even if Blanche was there, which he knew was not the case as ownership or even access to a small motor launch was not part of his family's assets, it would have been very difficult to spot her. By 10.00am the ever-reliable northeast wind had not arrived which meant the harbour was still glassy. Calm water made it comfortable for both those leaving and the families in the tiny boats below. Notes of farewell and love between the small launches and the Osterley were sent and returned on paper. The notes were placed in a slit made in a raw potato and thrown through the air. The R.M.S Osterley sailed at 11.00am on Saturday 10 February and forty minutes later, as Bert passed through Sydney Heads, he said his own silent farewell to his beloved family and homeland.

The first impression Bert had once on the boat, was the smell. It lingered and was always there no matter which part of the ship he was in. Being an engineer in his civilian life his work often had him immersed in oils, chemicals and grime however, onboard the Osterley the odors were at times, overwhelming. The combination of smoke, bitumen, seawater, and fuel was unique to ships. Unfortunately for the 4000 onboard another smell joined the party on a much too regular basis. Sanitation was a real problem. The Osterley was not designed as a troop carrier. A cargo of over 4000 soldiers had to be fed and cleaned. This caused some obvious problems. It took only a week for the complaints to begin. On or about Saturday 17 February a request came down from the Sanitary Sergeant Arthur W. Lane[29] that a sanitation squad needed to be formed to help alleviate "the bloody stench of shit" as Bert's mate Georgie Moore most eloquently stated.

---

left London for Melbourne, Sydney, and Brisbane via Suez. With the outbreak of war she was requisitioned as a troop transport, came through the war unscathed and returned to commercial service in Jan.1919. She led a comparatively uneventful life and was eventually broken up in Glasgow in 1930.
[29] Arthur W. Lane Sanitary Sergeant R.M.S 'Osterley as stated in ship's extract 26.2.17.

Georgie, Hughey, Bert and a couple of other blokes were quite prepared to help, thus the 'Sanitation Squad' came about.[30] Initially it was a matter of just buckets and mops but after a while Bert realized a new system had to be put into place. Changes needed to be made. As an engineer, Bert was a problem solver. Wider outlet pipes, more 's-bends' and the introduction of sea water as the primary flushing agent alleviated the stench. He decided to address the cause rather than fix the mess. Bert's first and only army recommendation during his time as a soldier would be based on Shit! Anyhow, this is how his citation read:

> *"The Commander R.M.S. 'Osterley' wishes to express his appreciation of the work of the Sanitary Squad, by this publication in Ship's orders. The Commanding Officer desires to associate himself with this appreciation: the work is excellent."[31]*

The non-commissioned slept on hammocks fastened to ceiling hooks, some of which looked very 'flimsy' when viewed with some of the bigger fellows camped beneath them. The bigger the seas got, the more the hammocks swung – but none ever came crashing down.

Being in the Sanitary Squad, Hughey and Bert had temporary access to all areas. In the officers' mess, above the commander's seat at the table, a framed gazetted citation caught Bert's attention. As a source of motivation to any who stood before it, the gilded frame was captioned: *'Burton VC., Dunstan VC., Tubb VC, 7th Infantry Battalion'*. The citation from the London Gazette dated 15 October 1915 read:

> *'For most conspicuous bravery at Lone Pine Trenches, on the 9 August 1915. In the early morning the enemy made a determined counterattack on the centre of the newly captured trench held by Lieutenant Tubb, Corporals Burton, Dunstan and a few men. They advanced up a sap*

---

[30] Extracted from Ship's order no. 17 dated 26.2.17 by Lieut. Colonel F.B.Heritage onboard Commander of Troops.
[31] Citation signed and dated by S.M.De Ravin, Captain, 26.2.17.

and blew in a sandbag barricade, leaving only one foot of it standing, but Lieutenant Tubb, with the two Corporals, repulsed the enemy and rebuilt the barricade. Supported by strong bombing parties, the enemy twice again succeeded in blowing in the barricade, but on each occasion, they were repulsed and the barricade rebuilt, although Lieutenant Tubb was wounded in the head and arm and Corporal Burton was killed by a bomb whilst most gallantly building up the parapet under a hail of bombs.'[32]

As Bert read this, he stood in quiet reflection wondering from where these three men found their bravery. All awarded the VC on the same day, same battle, together. One dead, one wounded. Were they born with it? What does it take to stare down the enemy and kill them? An answer never came to Bert although, internally, he did concede to himself that he would do anything for his soldier mates knowing full well that the same would be returned. The citation in front of him validated his notion of 'mateship.'

A couple of weeks into the trip the 1st Battalion, 24th Reinforcements had their first casualty. A young lad, whom Bert had no acquaintance, died of pneumonia. He was given the most terrific funeral at sea with full honors. However, Bert's sorrow and concern did not lie with this dead boy – all he could think about was this young fella's family back home. He was too young to be married so at the very least his parents were soon to be confronted with what no parent deserves – the death of their child. Bert knew too well that a next-of-kin will be informed by telegram usually delivered by the district priest or army representative. Bert wondered how Blanche would cope if confronted with the same news. A solemn and depressing thought for Bert considering it was his birthday. Bert turned 37 on Sunday 11 March on board the Osterley.

Later in March, the Osterley made Durban, South Africa. This was an exciting time for Bert and the rest of the contingent. The boredom, the constant rolling of the ship and the endless ocean horizon were starting to cause frustrations amongst the ranks. They desperately needed a break ashore to do what young

---

[32] Department of Veterans' Affairs, (2025), *William Dunstan*, DVA ANZAC Portal.

Aussies do. Unfortunately, due to misbehaving soldiers on earlier transports, the port commander was reluctant to allow shore leave for anyone. A compromise was reached; half the troops were given the first 24 hours leave and the remainder were 'released' for the second 24 hours.

The Port of Durban, being the transit hub between Australia, Europe and Asia was bustling not only with troop carriers but also supply and hospital ships. The city accommodated the transitting Australian soldiers with concerts and refreshments. The YMCA was always busy running their refreshment centre in the town's centre. Sight-seeing done, Bert and the rest re-embarked the Osterley, this time for the final leg. A farewell gesture to the troops from the docks was a song organized by the 'Angel of Durban' Miss Ethal Campbell.[33] She greeted every Australian troopship arriving and departing the Port of Durban with gifts and newspapers. Back on board it didn't take long to be fully reacquainted with oil fumes and the endless roll of the Atlantic.

The food was quite acceptable whilst in transit to England. Always hot and plenty of it. The only reason for complaint was the lack of variation. As they crossed the equator, unbeknown to most on board, it was the norm for a celebration of sorts. To commemorate this naval ritual the mess prepared an 'Equator-Crossing' feast complete with menu.[34] The larrikin humor of those kitchen boys was highly evident in the menu prepared especially for the occasion. The menu consisted of dishes such as *Consommé a la Rubbish, Sauté de la Suffolk Lingo, Curried Rabbit Alf-onso, Underdun Roast Sirloin of Beef minus Yorko, Roast Head of Pork Quick Style, Stuffed Mutton not Dinkum, Roast Turkey a la Perhaps.*

Even though they were rarely seen, the R.M.S Osterley was escorted by several troop destroyers and other transport ships separated by approximately one sailing day duration. In January 1917, Germany reengaged their naval tactic of unrestricted submarine

---

[33] Miss Campbell received a Member of the Most Excellent Order of the British Empire (MBE) in 1919 for her work during the First World War. As well as distributing gifts to soldiers at Durban port, Miss Campbell arranged entertainment for the troops in Durban.
[34] Retrieved from http://www.australiansatwar.gov.au/stories/stories.asp?war=W1&id=33. It was originally the 1915 Christmas menu for the 'T.S. Suffolk' and was modified to suit this author's needs.

warfare. All allied boats, military or merchant, were fair game according to the Huns. Consequently, this placed all non-escorted ships in peril. A rumor flew through the fleet of a cholera outbreak and that was all it took for the ship's M.O., short for medical Officer but often referred to as the 'Quack', to get out the needle, again. So, with a swipe of iodine and a quick jab, another inoculation was done with. Bert was under the impression that he had already been 'fixed up' against cholera. Apparently, the 'quack' did not agree.

One of the major challenges on board the ship was boredom. Bert would often wish for something to happen. Regular church services and concerts broke the routine army drills, still the days were long. Boxing matches were very popular, but participation never appealed to Bert due to the fact he couldn't box and getting hit in the face was not that appealing. He was short, cranky and like his mate back home Dessey, couldn't fight very well. "Best leave the boxing to the younger boys is a smart decision," Bert thought to himself.

Other activities were put together to keep everyone occupied and to the relieve the boredom. Sports competitions such as obstacle races, egg and spoon races, and pillow fights provided healthy competition between the men. Still, it was the boxing that gained the most interest, especially the country boys. Bert did not have much success at any of the sporting challenges. The fact that he was almost 20 years older than most probably had something to do with it. As the Osterley motored north it became hotter and more humid. The evenings brought a welcomed respite to the heat.

Two months to the day, 10 April 1917,[35] English soil was sighted. The Osterley was moored 1000 yards off Portsmouth amongst a flotilla of naval destroyers, colliers, lighters and transports, all flying the White Ensign. First thing the next day disembarkation was undertaken with a sense of urgency. It seemed that the waterways were in the middle of a massive troop transfer. Bert was later told that it involved the movement of 80,000 troops in 10 days through the port. Everybody was particularly grateful to get ashore. Kits were packed in record time. Bert and the boys didn't waste time and were amongst the first in line to clamber

---

[35] Date taken from A.H.Menere's Army Form B. 103 Casualty Form – Active Service.

down to the awaiting small troop transports. There were a dozen or so of these boats each with a carry capacity of 50 men plus kit so, the process took a while. "Why couldn't the Osterley moor at the docks like the other troop carries?" was the overriding sentiment of the 24th Reinforcements as they struggled on and off the troop transports. The harbour port of Southampton was a sight, but nothing compared to the soldiers' own Sydney Harbour.

Chapter 7
Arrival The Mother Country

We stand on the shores of Durban,
And watch the transports go.
To England from Australia,
Hurrying to and fro.
Bearing the men of a nation,
Who are heroes to the core.
To stand and fall by the Motherland,
And they're sending thousands more!

Extract from poem 'Australia', author unknown.
Diggers' Poems by Returned Soldiers.

Getting off the Osterley transport ship and onto dry land did not happen as quickly as Bert wanted. They were moored offshore from Portsmouth waiting their turn to enter the Southhampton Waterway. As they waited, ships by the hundreds navigated past. Munition ships, hospital ships, troop carriers, civilian and armed forces alike made the waterway look like an afternoon rush in Pitt Street. Blimps littered the sky. This was the first time Bert had seen anything like it. Occasionally, British airplanes would pass overhead in formation on their way to do their bit. Finally, the Osterley's anchors were raised, and the familiar grind of the propellers could be heard. As the ship approached the harbour, it was taken under the charge of a military tug which towed it through the narrow waters of the entrance to the harbour and directed it to its assigned anchorage point.

The smaller transports unloaded troops, supplies, horses, munitions and other various pieces of war-time hardware from the Osterley with amazing efficiency. Some boats moored directly on the docks, but not the Osterley. For the troops of the 24th small troop transports ferried over 4000 soldiers to land. Bert sensed that there was an air of urgency in getting the 24th reinforcements on land and into the action. In Bert's eyes, Southampton was certainly holding its reputation as the Gateway to War. For centuries the port was the trade gate to and from other lands across the seas. It experienced Viking raids and was the port of entry for the Norman Conquest of 1066. That was the beginning of the town's prosperity.[36]

Twenty-four hours a day the same cycle would repeat itself. Unfortunately, as the boats were unloaded, they were then reloaded with the by-products of war – the wounded. The soldiers going home were not as complete as those arriving. Missing limbs was a common affliction. These poor fellows had been hospitalized, fixed up and now confronted with an uncertain future. There were no corpses. It was common knowledge that you would be buried on the field on which you fell. Bert was quite ambivalent towards this notion. The manpower and the logistics needed to relocate the fallen back home to Australia would be beyond that which was available. The notion of being buried next to those who bore the same burden and paid the same price was quite comforting to Bert.

On the first night the troops bivvied in the Southampton Town Common. Billets were unavailable. Southampton was the Allies' gateway to this war. The harbour was deep enough to handle the shipping and the town big enough to handle the troops. The locals provided for the troops in magnificent fashion. A network of volunteer women was organised and on call to assist with meals, tea and basic comforts whilst the established cottage industry took advantage of relieving many a soldier's pay on mementos and minor necessities. A total of 8,149,685 troops and their equipment departed for mainland Europe through the port during the war years.[37]

Before boarding the train to Durrington training camp, Bert and a few of the boys used some of the free time to explore. The 'Chine' was visited and made good use of. Also known as

---

[36] Southampton's prosperity was assured following the Norman Conquest in 1066, when it became the major port of transit between Winchester (the capital of England until the early 12th century) and Normandy.
[37] Rance, Adrian (1986). Southampton. An Illustrated History. Milestone. *ISBN 0-903852-95-0*.

St Mark's Soldiers' Rest, the Chine was not only a tearoom-style meeting place for couples and soldiers, but it also provided other services. A photo studio was in full swing taking portraits of soldiers for keepsakes and perhaps used as a personalised post card to be sent home. Bert had his photo portrait taken and later used it to compliment the cushion cover[38] he was to commission for Blanche when visiting Etaples later in September. Another service the Chine provided was letter writing. Many soldiers of the A.I.F. were not particularly competent in the written form of the English language and took advantage of this service when sending home postcards from Southampton.

On a full stomach of porridge, beef and tea their marching skills were put to the test the next day. Thus, the boys set out in formation and marched to the train station.[39] It was a relatively short train trip of 45 miles (70 km), so Bert and the crew were settled by evening. On arrival at Durrington Camp the 24th reinforcements of the 1st Battalion were directed to their accommodation and thus the 8-week training began.

The Battalion's first impression of the camp was not good. The camp was overcrowded and many of the incoming men were accommodated in tents which could be seen on the outer perimeter of the camp – row after row. Everything was drab with no colour. The 24th Battalion was more fortunate. Bert and the boys were to be housed in the barracks. Again, row after row of barracks displaying an air of organisation and regulation. It was a self-contained township with shops, theatres, bakeries and a post-office. The roads were terrible. The constant summer rains created a glutinous slurry of mud which found its way into every aspect of the new recruits' army life. The endless transit of vehicles compounded the problem. Boots, socks and jocks always had an element of mud embedded somewhere. To address the situation the engineers laid down fine white clay in the hope of absorbing some of the water and hardening up the slurry. It made little difference

---

[38] The cushion cover is in the possession of the Ward family. It is the only war-time memento that exists within this part of Henri Menere's family tree and was the catalyst behind this book.
[39] In 1916, the AIF decided to form Australian training battalions in England from which reinforcements could be posted to Australian Divisions in France. As well, Battalions that were already formed, such as the 1st, did their acclimatization and final training at the Salisbury Plain. Camps were established at Larkhill, Rolleston, Durrington, Perham Downs, Parkhouse and Tidworth. However, Larkhill seems to have been particularly unpopular with the Australians.

and resulted in white mud everywhere as opposed to black. The fortunate thing for the 24th Battalion was that they would be long gone before the winter set in and turned the mud to ice and frozen sludge. Training started immediately.

As the weeks passed, news of the front and what was happening back home started to filter through. Generally, home front news arrived about 10 weeks after the event. News from the front filtered through much quicker. Word of mouth was much faster than printed fact. Late in June, Bert and the troops at Durrington were buoyed by the fact that the first American troops had finally reached the French coast.[40] Many of the reinforcing troops were concerned that it would all be over before they got the chance to give the Hun the belting they deserved. Bert's thoughts were anything but! "The quicker this war ends, the quicker the killing stops and the sooner I will be back at home living the blessed life". He missed the hugs of his daughters, the smell of their hair, and the warmth of their tiny bodies as they fell asleep in his arms. A conflict of emotions was always tearing and pulling at Bert. Non-the-less, he was where he had to be. There was no turning back.

---

[40] June 27th, 1917. The first American troops reached France led by Major General 'Black Jack' Pershing, Chronicle of the 20th Century, p228.

Chapter 8

Transferred to the 62nd Battalion: Goodbye George and Hughey.

See ya mate!
T'was tough but a laugh,
Durrington's a shit hole,
Thank heavens it's passed.

They're splittin' us up mate!
We're together no more.
When I'm back from Belgium,
I'll give you a call.

'See ya Mate!' by Brandt 2025

The 1st Battalion, 24th reinforcements began to disperse pretty much straight away. High command began battalion transfers on a basis of strategy and statistical prediction. Even though friendships were new, mateship within the ranks developed quickly. Saying goodbye to mates under a cloud of uncertainty was always tough. Bert never saw Hughey Lowe or George Moore again after 28 April 1917. On this day Bert was formally transferred to the 62nd Battalion[41] as part of the newly formed AIF 6th Division. Relocated from Durrington to Windmill Hill, still within the Salisbury Plain precinct, was part of the transfer. The training

---

[41] The 62nd battalion was formed 16th September 1917 as a foundation component of the 6th Australian Division. However, the division was quickly disbanded due to lack of manpower resulting from losses in France and the democratic failure of the conscription vote back home on the 28 October 1917. Hence, Albert Menere's subsequent transfer to the 3rd Division, 35th Battalion on 1 September 1917.

camps encompassed approximately 20 square kilometres. Camps existed within camps. Hospitals, stores, cinemas; a city built specifically for the training of soldiers. Some of the welfare stores were Bollen's Fruit Stores, Vallers & Co, newsagents, Sergeant's Empire Stores and Restaurant, the YMCA, The Salvation Army, the Military Cinema, and the 1200 bed Fargo Hospital, built in 1915, north of Fargo plantation.[42]

A total of thirty-four individual infantry training camps, each capable of housing a battalion, were constructed and used by all arms of the British and A.I.F. armies. Buildings consisted mostly of wooden huts with corrugated tin rooves. The whole camp seemed to be made of timber and tin, even the church and cinema were made of corrugated iron. When it rained, which seemed to be always, you could hardly have a conversation over the rain beating down on the tin roof.

The next twelve weeks Bert felt alone. There were other blokes about, and new acquaintances being made, but he missed his family. This was the real deal, and he knew that he had to lift mentally and physically to get through it. Troops were coming and going, transfers from one battalion to another with minimal notice given was the norm. Bert didn't receive many letters from home, this made him feel despondent at times, but he wasn't alone. Homesickness was rife throughout the troops.

The roads of Windmill Hill Camp were no different than those of Durrington Camp. The new roads at Windmill Hill were put together by the Royal Engineers. Again, they were constructed from the natural chalk of Salisbury Plain. The chalk was everywhere. It proved sticky when wet and expelled itself in clouds of white dust when dry. Nearly impossible to walk on and nothing ever stayed dry. One of Bert's letters home to Blanche reflected the following sentiment that read something like this:

'It has been raining like fun here and things about Windmill Hill are pretty sloppy. It's a rotten place when it rains and a jolly sight worse if it keeps fine for any length

---

[42] James, NDG, 1987, Plain Soldiering – a history of the armed forces on Salisbury Plain, Hobnob, Salisbury, 094618039.

of time. The dust is that fine that it will get in anywhere; do what you can, you can't get away from it.'[43]

"Bloody hell, what a difference from the drought conditions back in Corowa," Bert thought to himself as he 'sludged' his way to the cinema one evening. He wondered if he would ever see blue sky again. No wonder the Pommy's were regarded as a whinging miserable bunch back home. During the coldest and bleakest of days, Bert often reminisced growing up in the bush. If he was asked what he missed the most about his early days in the bush, chances are it would be his mum's rabbit stew and the afternoon quiet. They were good days, hard, but good. He thought about his mother often and the life she was now living with her new husband. His mother Elizabeth, married soon after the death of Bert's father and at the age of 32 years she became Mrs Elizabeth Bartlett. Bert never did warm to Henry Bartlett, but he did look after his mother. That was enough.

As the weeks of induction and training progressed, Bert started to feel more comfortable with many of the fellows in the 62nd. The comradery was building. It was a real melting pot of ragtag, dusty, country-bred, professional and worker types. Despite where you came from, how many acres the family owned, or how much schooling you had, one thing was for sure – you were part of a unit and ready to look after each other no matter what. Bert's Lee-Enfield .303 rifle was a good friend and as his training progressed, he felt very comfortable with it by his side.

In formation on the parade ground, on what was an unusually warm and dry English day, the Commanding Officer announced that the 62nd Battalion was to be dismantled and reassigned. Bert was again to be transferred. Word was that the newly formed 6th Division was being dissolved, and its soldiers redistributed to reinforce other divisions, primarily the 3rd Division. This could have been upsetting but most of the lads were transferred together. The A.I.F.'s 9th Brigade, 35th Battalion[44] was to be Bert's new battalion.

---

[43] On 3rd September 1916, W.J Sinney of the 42nd Battalion wrote, in an unpublished letter from Salisbury Plains.
[44] The 35th Battalion was originally formed in December 1915 in Newcastle, New South Wales. The bulk of the battalion's recruits was drawn from the Newcastle region and thus it was dubbed

The 62nd Battalion's last march out was on Friday 23 August 1917. Bert and the boys left for France to reinforce the AIF's 3rd Division on the Belgium front. This was it! It wouldn't be until 1 September 1917 that his transfer to the 35th Battalion would be official.

Friday morning witnessed the reinforcements, still the 62nd Battalion, departure from Salisbury Plain. After chafing for months under the routine of drill and exercise, a battalion at last emerged as a smart, well equipped, well-trained fighting unit, with every man fit and eager to go head-to-head with the enemy. Sniping, hand-to-hand fighting, and dealing with gas was a part of each soldier's skill base. "It's OK practicing these skills but what about when it gets real?" Bert once again asked himself.

Reveille was sounded at 4.30am. It was a cold, bleak morning when they had their last breakfast at the camp. After the meal, a period of tremendous hustle and bustle ensued. There was the strapping and unstrapping of equipment, the packing of kits, and the struggles to get all personal possessions, gear, rations, blankets and utensils securely packed. Each soldier's kit weighed approximately 100lbs (45kg), exclusive of rifles. Bert's pack was typical in that it contained the following:

> '1 overcoat, socks, 1 towel, 1 flannel shirt, 1 holdall,[45]
> 1 thick blanket, 1 waterproof coat, one waterproof sheet,
> 1 pair of drawers, 1 sheepskin vest, soap, razor, knife,
> fork, spoon, 1 mess tin, iodine, dressings, handkerchief,
> and other small nicknacks and tucker for 24 hrs, writing
> material and water bottle full, abdomen belt, balaclava
> cap, muffler and gloves. In addition to this the soldiers
> had to wear 1 tunic, 1 pants, 1 pair drawers, 2 shirts,
> 1 hat, 2 pairs of socks, 1 pair heavy boots, 1 cardigan
> jacket, and 1 muffler.'[46]

'Newcastle's Own'. Reflecting the demographics of the area, there was a high proportion of miners among the battalion's original members. The 35th Battalion became part of the 9th Brigade of the 3rd Australian Division. It left Sydney, bound for the United Kingdom in May 1916. Arriving there in early July, the battalion spent the next four months training. It crossed to France in late November and moved into the trenches of the Western Front for the first time on 26 November 1916 just in time for the onset of the terrible winter of 1916–17.

[45] Sometimes referred to as a 'housewife' containing needles, cotton and buttons.

[46] Extract from pack inventory of Alfred Jonn Hayes, 2328, 36th Battalion, Clark, p52.

At length the reinforcing battalion fell in for final inspection, then departed on the four-mile journey to Amesbury Railway Station, gaily marching to the strains of the 'Colonel Bogie March' played by the battalion band. The band was not very good.

The troops left Amesbury on three trains which arrived at Folkstone at 11am, noon and 2pm on their way to play their part in the mud, sleet and horror of the Western Front. Of course, the exact destination was not known, but in his heart, Bert knew it was going to be frightful. In large sheds next to the wharf, Bert and the boys were kept waiting until nightfall. As usual, the food was plentiful. During the long hours that elapsed they consumed buns and cakes, vast quantities of chocolate, fruit, chewing gum and other edibles which were purchased at the canteens in the sheds. They smoked cigarettes and drank a lot, not all tea. This was the only relief they got during the tedious and monotonous afternoon and evening.

At last, the long wait came to an end and the battalion gladly received, and cheerfully obeyed, the order to "fall in." Embarkation on the channel transports started at 8 p.m. and the passage was rough. Many of the lads, including Bert, displaced all the food they had eaten into the murky cold waters of the English Channel. The French coastal port of Rouelle was reached early the following morning Friday 24 August 1917.

Disembarkation took place at midday amid a blanket of freezing cold rain. Despite the weather, many French civilians turned out to welcome the new contingent of AIF troops. "At last," Bert thought. A chance to use his French phrasebook[47] purchased back at Windmill Hill. He and some of the others shouted in French telling them that the war would soon be over now that they had arrived. The townsfolk just stared and made no reply. It seemed to Bert that they did not understand their own language! A long trying hill at the end of a six-mile march ushered the battalion into the so called 'Rest Camp'.

What a desolate scene met their eyes, again. The ground oozed with mud and rows of discoloured sodden tents, dripping and leaking, offering a very dubious, low level of shelter. The first night

---

[47] This French book being part of the inventory returned to and signed for by Blanche Menere dated 13th Sept. 1918.

out from England was spent in an uninviting atmosphere of gloom and dejection and it was with much pleasure that the 62nd and the rest of the reinforcing battalions left Rouelle. Whilst Bert and the other reinforcement troops journeyed into the heartland of battle, the original 35th Battalion was in training at Wismes in the Campagne-de- Boulonnais area of France, west of the Belgium boarder and the Hindenburg Line. Bert was on his way to join them.

Chapter 9

To France: Albert steps up to become a Stretcher Bearer.

"Just a human mortal he appears to be,
A soldier garbed in drab khaki,
Distinguished by armband – letters 'S.B.'
He's our Stretcher Bearer.

Thro' fierce barrage and death-dealing shell,
He snatches the maimed from the jaws of hell,
Of grim sights he sees he ne'r will tell-
Our brave Stretcher bearer."

Extract from 'Idle Moments in the Line',
Private J.M.Harkins, 23rd Battalion, 1919.

From disembarkation, the march to the railway station was mostly level or downhill and therefore easy. Bert spent the next 30 hours travelling by slow train, in horseboxes, which were marked "8 chevaux, 40 hommes". That meant the truck was supposed to accommodate either eight horses or forty men. They reached Etaples[48] in the Boulogne-Sur-Mer region at 3 o'clock on Tuesday afternoon then marched to the allocated muster area on the village perimeter. On arrival Bert and the boys were confronted with a town wrapped in a dense mantle of fog which reminded him of

---

[48] Étaples was a major British base depot and a significant training ground for the AIF. Troops received an additional 10 days of training there after completing initial training in England. This included a strict medical check and military tests, such as practicing gas attacks. By 1917, Etaples housed 100,000 troops and served as a hub for supplies, detention centres for prisoners, and a network of hospitals.

Corowa in winter. Waiting again in the cold, hunger and boredom had to be endured before billeting arrangements were completed. Bert was so tired he could have slept on a stone-brick floor that evening. His wish came true.

It was fortunate that Bert's group had two brothers who were both proficient in the French language. They acted as interpreters on many occasions and thus greatly facilitated smoothing out the difficulties in which they occasionally found themselves with the locals. It was a novelty to find themselves billeted in schools and halls, barns and out-houses; all in a state of disrepair. Everything was damp, but the eclectic mix of smells was interestingly pleasant. Food in France was very different to that of England and back home in Australia. In fact, the food was much better. It was amazing what the French locals could prepare with such limited supplies and rationing.

Ten days were spent in Etaples training and acclimatizing to the conditions. The training camp was huge and catered for New Zealand, Canadian, British and Scottish troops. It provided a specialized 10-day program focusing on health, fitness and fine-tuning frontline awareness. At any time 60-80 thousand troops were transitting. For Bert and the boys Etaples was a sight to see. Most being from the country, Etaples was a wonderland of distractions. The cottage industry was booming as was the pleasure industry. With pay in hand there were many opportunities for a lonely soldier to spend some money. Bert was fully aware that he did not want to take something home that he did not leave with, so he just humoured the younger lads as they went pleasure shopping. Bert spent some time at 'Madam's Estaminate' on Bois Boulevarde, an alcohol-serving café which suited his needs perfectly.

It was here in Etaples that Bert commissioned a local embroiderer to fashion a cushion cover for his dear wife Blanche.[49] Embroided onto the cushion cover was a message of love to his wife, the AIF insignia as well as the studio portrait of himself taken in Southhampton. Bert dispatched the completed memento from the base post office. He hoped it would reach his beloved back home in Australia.

Part of the training at Etaples included the use of the box-respirator. The instruction and re-instruction in its use went on and on for good reason which would become evident in the very

---

[49] See Appendix 1. This was the item that ignited the author's need to tell Albert Menere's story.

near future. The respirator provided protection from the gasses used by the enemy on and behind the front lines. They looked a weird lot with the masks on. Their faces completely encased in rubber with glass covered apertures to see through. Obtaining air happened via a snake-like tube attached to the respirator. The term 'box-respirator' was soon corrupted into 'Gasp-irater.' Night operations, musketry range practice, close-order drills and rifle exercises were repeated with continued regularity. The practice fitting of gas regulators could be commanded at any time, so every soldier needed to always carry his. Word from the front was that the Hun's use of gas was becoming more prevalent as the battle-field air became heavier and colder as the winter of 1917 approached. The ten-day program completed, those of the now dissolved 62nd battalion were officially 'Taken on Strength' and reassigned to the 35th battalion.

It was during the final days at Etaples that Bert and others stepped forward and agreed to reskill as stretcher bearers (S.B). He was teamed with three others and drilled in protocol and procedures associated with that of the S.B. Bert knew that the survival prospects for stretcher bearers were not good, but it was something he was comfortable with.

The protocol for the stretcher bearer was simple; leave your Lee Enfield behind and in teams of two, recover the wounded from the field. They would go out at night and during breaks in the fighting. They had to overcome shell craters, crowded trenches, barbed wire, bogs and bodies. Night-time retrievals would be particularly hazardous. Traversing to the assigned destination, they would run like crazy and then freeze as a star shell illuminated the skies. When it extinguished, they would again run in the dark until the next flare did its job and lit up anything that moved under the illuminations. This cycle of stop and go, coupled with the mud and debris could add hours onto the stretcher bearers' task.

Priority one retrieve the wounded, priority two retrieve the dead. During the winter of 1917 because of the mud, a stretcher bearer needed to team up with three others to do the job. The mud was knee deep at times and what would normally be a two-man quick retrieval process, could take hours. When this happened the risk of injury or death increased significantly. The stretcher bearers would transport the wounded and dead to either the Regimental Aid Post or the Dressing Station located in the reserve trenches.

Chapter 10
Meanwhile at Messines.

The Battle of Messines took place between 7 July and 14 July 1917. Bert was yet to join the 35th Battalion and was still part of the 62nd Battalion training in England at this time. The significance of this battle and the 35th Battalion's contribution need to be highlighted. Casualties to the 35th during Messines Offensive: 5 officers, 431 other ranks.

'Newcastle's Own', the 35th Battalion, participated in the Battle of Messines. According to British strategists, this was a critical battle with its primary objective to gain control of the elevated ridge. This would secure a visual offensive advantage from Ypres in the north to the elevated vantage points of Passchendaele in the northeast. If successful, the German 4th army would be deprived of this tactical position. As part of the 9th and 10th Brigades' contingent, the 35th Battalion was sent in on day one as part of the first objective. This was the first major offensive that the AIF's newly formed 3rd Division would take part. The offensive started with the detonation of 19 mines beneath the German lines. The mines were detonated at zero hour, 3.10am.

"The largest mine on the front was close to us – containing 20 tons of gun cotton … Our first warning that she was fired was by sounds like distant rumblings of thunder – then gradually getting closer – then directly to our front the earth was seen to be rising like a huge mushroom – suddenly to be flung into space with an awe-inspiring roar and the earth trembled, to me it appeared as if with mingled fear and relief – fear of the dread power she had stored in her bowels, relief because it had vented its fury and

although she was sadly torn, its menace was gone. The mine made a crater 300 feet wide by 90 feet deep." [50]

Prior to zero hour the 36th Battalion was to act as a carrying party in support of the other battalions of the 9th Brigade. This was an extremely dangerous task which involved moving forwards and then backwards supplying and resupplying the advancing troops with picks, shovels, munitions and ammunition. It involved carrying their loads in Yukon packs and slings, exposing themselves in the open under heavy fire, gas and high explosive bombardments. Post detonation, the 36th continued with the resupplying of the front line with such efficiency it was noted in official war diary records that: *'After zero-hour goods reports continued to come acknowledging the efficiency of our carrying parties and the determination with which they plodded through the enemy barrage time and time again with requirements for the front line.'* [51]

The resulting craters cleared the way for the advance. The 35th was presented with the dead, dazed and mutilated. Those enemies not disabled were still in the fight. Before the detonation the Huns dispensed gas which played havoc on those advancing, however, a consequence of the underground detonations dispensed the gas back towards what was left of the German trenches. The explosion was noted as the largest ever detonated up to that time. The following is another soldier's account of what went down in the early hours of 7 June 1917. [52]

> *"At about 11.30 pm on 6 June, me and the boys left our bivouac site near the Kruisstraat and in cold sheeting rain commenced the march to the assembly area. The mobilization started as we passed through the supply stations and field hospitals it seemed that all others, me included, were a little more cheerful than one would expect under these circumstances; what with the mud, rain, and the fact we were heading into the pit that was the front line. The noise of war was constant but muffled. There was no doubt we were getting closer to the lines because the concussion from the high explosives (H.E.s) was increasing.*

---

[50] As reported by Captain Robert Cuthbert Grieve VC, AIF 37th Battalion.
[51] AWM Official war Diaries 36th Battalion June 1917.
[52] A fictitious soldier created by the author.

As midnight approached the air became misty and acrid. The smell of lyddite generated by the HE bombardment stung my lungs. I was hoping it wasn't the dreaded gas.

There were thousands of troops in transit, not all seemed to be going in the same direction. At one stage we were held up for 45 minutes whilst companies of the 25th Battalion passed along the front of our line of troops. Robbie Drew, Georgie Salter and Bill Campbell were directly in front and behind me. No one spoke, just listened. Eventually, and after much swearing and complaining by the younger lads further to the front, our column began to move once again. With a mile to go before the front line proper, several of Fritz's gas shells burst near us impeding our progress. Everyone had to stop and don gas masks. My unfounded optimism of avoiding the dreaded gas was quickly dismissed. The track marked '9th Brigade', which was us, became increasingly heavy and I felt sorry for the men in the carrying party weighed down with stores and munitions. I would normally have offered help, but a strong sense of self-preservation now existed, and my only focus was to at least get through this, my first major battle, alive. We reached our designated assembly tapes at about 1.00am on the morning of Saturday 7 June 1917 and were immediately shelled. The sporadic shelling created some disorganization, and several were killed or wounded. One blast dropped about 10 yards from me but due to the thick concentration of men, the blast was absorbed by those around me. To my surprise I was not scared. My buddies Robbie, George and Bill were still upright and in relative fine fettle. I had a job to do, and my battalion mates depended on me as I depended on them. The more intense the shelling became, the angrier I got. I surprised myself with this emotion, but emotions are something I had little control over at this time. For the next couple of hours, we waited. The shelling settled down and things got a bit quieter as if something was on the cusp of happening. The flares diminished in number, and for a time, darkness enveloped everything. A little after 3.00am hell beyond the ridge opened its arms.

The officers and their NCOs did a marvellous job keeping the troops focused and calm and in no time the battalion was sent 'over the top' surging ahead towards the carnage and craters. The dead were everywhere. The disabled and bewildered Hun unable to comprehend the enormity of what just took place. But there were still pockets of resistance with pillboxes and some frontline German trenches still in tack. We still had a job to do.

The camaraderie I felt on that night was strong; we fought as one. It was expected that in the 35th that no one gets left behind – if you take a hit be it fatal or not, rest assured that a fellow 'thirty-fiver' will be there for you. I realized on this night that to die for your mates would be OK. Not leaving anyone behind was an optimistic sentiment held by most. Realizing this on the battlefield was near impossible. A special bond exists in battle and this bond is emblazoned with selfless courage. I knew that I would do my duty, not for the King, not for Australia but for those blokes standing next to me on this night in the mud and rain.

Within the first eighty yards the 5th and 6th platoons encountered a German machine-gun post raking the front of the nearby 10th Battalion. I was 30 yards behind the initial assault with three other lads waiting for the inevitable. This one pillar box had pinned me and dozens from both the 35th, 11th, and 10th. I did not know the full particulars until a few days later but a Lieutenant G.H. Leaver, in a true act of selfless heroism, took the initiative.

Lieutenant G.H. Leaver[53] was a platoon commander in the 10th and got around behind the pillbox and was almost at the machine gun when a German soldier with a revolver

[53] Lieutenant Leaver was a platoon commander in one of two specially trained Storm Companies and so when the battalion encountered a pillbox on the morning of 20 September, Leaver was ordered to take his platoon forward and deal with it. With a German machine-gunner holding up the advance by raking the front of the 11th Battalion swift action needed to be taken so Lieutenant Leaver quickly got around behind the pillbox and was almost at the machine gun when a German with a revolver shot him in the head. It was only a fortnight earlier Lieutenant Leaver celebrated his 21st birthday.

shot him in the head. It was later reported that Leaver's men 'went mad'. Corporal Hodge of the 11th Battalion rushed forward, shot the machine-gunner and captured the gun. The Germans tried to surrender but the men stormed the place with fierce determination and no compassion. The average solder does not enjoy killing but I suppose, in the heat of the moment, and filled with an emotional cocktail of anger, fear and resentment, many an action can be internally justified in war.

My initiation into the black heartlessness of war happened. Another German machine-gun pillbox lay to the south of the initial crater and was manned by several Huns. We had just been shelled, gassed and fired upon and many of us, me included, saw mates torn apart from red hot shrapnel and bullets from Fritz's MG 08/15 machine guns. Our rush towards Fritz was unstoppable and the enemy had nowhere to hide. Their trench fronts weren't that high and were easily breached. The rush was on. I remember being keenly aware that not only Fritz occupied theses trenches, but so did our own advancing diggers. "Shit, I hope I don't shoot a cobber" grunted one of the lads behind me as we both tripped 'arse over' down some flimsy crates Fritz had used to prop himself up. This fellow spat out exactly what I was thinking. This was the closest most of the boys from the 35th had been to the enemy and I knew that at any moment 'close' would become 'face to face'.

I think I killed a man that night. I did not see his face; I only saw him fall. I did not go back for a second look. It was exhilarating, it was terrifying, it had to be done. I shot him in the head; he dropped without a murmur. It was surprisingly easy and just as easily, it could have gone another way. We were surrounded by blood, death, mud, noise and fire and at that moment I knew that I would hold onto these visions forever, whether I wanted to or not. With the enemy pillbox position successfully taken it was time for the stretcher bearers to step up and do their job. They assessed the situation immediately. There was half a dozen wounded scattered behind us at about 50 yards. The stretcher *bearers were not far behind the initial push. They were amazing and relentless in doing their job. Normally it would take two stretcher bearers to carrier one wounded out but because of the knee-deep mud created by the explosions, it required one on each corner of the stretcher to keep it balanced and at the same time make progress back through shell holes and displaced barbed wire to the casualty station. Once there, the unfortunate lads were dropped off and the SBs would turn around and start over again. In my mind they are the toughest and are all heroes. It was a long night, but the objective was achieved and set the scene for our victory at Messines which would be declared on 14 June 1917."*

Chapter 11

Taken on Strength to Ypres and onto Belgium.

Not comin' back to-night matey,
And the reliefs are comin' through.
We're all goin' out all right, matey,
Only we're leaving you.

Gawd! It's a bloody sin, matey,
Now that we've finished the fight.
We go when the reliefs come in, matey,
But you're stayin' here to-night.

Chum o' mine and your dead, matey,
And this is the way we part.
The bullet went through your head, matey,
But gawd! It went through my 'eart.

Extract from the poem 'Matey (Cambrin, 1915)',
Patrick MacGill.[54]

On Sunday 2 September 1917, the official 'march to the front' began for Bert and the 9th Infantry Brigade. All battalions were included. Etaples was left behind. Twenty-seven miles (44kms) to the northwest was Wismes, the battalions' next destination just shy of the Ypres sector and the front line. Arriving there late in the afternoon, Bert and the boys were billeted in a cotton factory in Rue Principale with their headquarters in Rue des Ecoles. The distant

---

[54] From Poetryexplorer.net, sourced 17.5.25.

thud of artillery was not as muffled. The smell of cordite was stronger and the hum of overhead planes, some friendly, some not, was constant. Command indicated that the chance of an artillery hit was not likely, but it wasn't ruled out. "Be alert boys, be alert!" was shouted down the line as they marched.

As Bert and the Brigade progressed the sad colourless panorama of war was becoming clearer. The roads were busy and pushed to the side were the broken consequences of earlier battles. The trees that were still standing were stripped bare of limbs and leaves. The broken wagons had the rotting corpses of their horses still bridled. What could not be retrieved of the goods being transported was left in the mud. The debris was as thick as the stench. Occasionally some of the locals would be on the road going about some form of normality amongst the swirl of despair. At a couple of the crossroads hessian mesh was swaying aloft lightly connected to what was left of the trees. Torn and shredded, they were no longer required to do what they were initially intended which was to screen troop movement from the Fritz observers on the hill. The battle front had since relocated.

Early September the Wismes Camp was bustling with the English, Canadians and of course, Aussies. The skill base for all soldiers had been previously established and now specialist training for those concerned would take place. Other than specialist training, time was filled with battalion activities and sport. Designed to maintain fitness and to consolidate teamwork, the competitive aspect of the activities was popular amongst the rank and file. From the third to the fifth of September the 9th Infantry Brigade held their group sports competitions. Consisting of transport and cooking challenges, the 35th battalion achieved first place in the Best Field Kitchen event held nearby at the village of Drionville. Bert and the others were quite pleased with this achievement, but the best was to come when they won the Brigade's mule competition.[55]

A two-day break on the coast was a welcomed relief for the 35th Battalion. Each battalion of the 9th Brigade was rostered a well-earned break from their battle preparations. On Sunday 16 September, Bert and the boys were transported in lorries to

---

[55] War Diaries for the 35th Battalion for the month of September 1917.

the coastal province of Tardinghem in the Pas-de-Calais region. A delightful hour drive to the west presented a magnificent French backdrop of high cliffs, pebbled beaches and blue skies. Bert had never seen a coastline like it. For two days he immersed himself in the village atmosphere which included wine and food. The cottage industry in Tardinghem was bolstered by the continual flow of itinerant soldiers enjoying organised recreation in this small village. The sales of chocolates, sweet-heart trinkets and custom embroided fabrics seemed to be the core industry. This was to be the last semblance of solace for the battalion before the uncertainty of the Belgium frontline.

Tardinghem consisted of a dozen or so cobbled streets and just as many earthen lanes. Most roads ran parallel to the sea; there was a lake to the north and the sea to the west. Bert had never witnessed a sun setting into the sea. He was happy on that afternoon. Bert and his mates took in the food and the red wine. The wine was a blessing because it softened the discomfort of tent accommodation in the field. Billeting was not an option due to the enormous numbers of itinerant soldiers. The night was spent amongst the earthen smells of damp canvas tents and tainted air, the result of a dozen men farting within the confines of a single tent. The night was fine but, in the distance, Bert could hear the dull thud of war. He knew it would soon be much closer. Earlier in the evening the 3rd Division's concert troop performed. The concert lasted two hours and was well received by all. Home-grown ballads were woven into an ensemble of well-rehearsed tunes. The 35th Battalion returned to Wismes at 8.00pm on Monday 17 September 1917. The next morning, they were confronted with more gas demonstrations and drills.

Training and preparations continued and on Monday 24 September 1917, the Brigade marched in full kit to Happe for inspection and a march past. The commander of the 9th Infantry Brigade was pleased with those under his command. The next day boot, feet and kit inspections were the final preparatory tasks undertaken prior to moving out. Foot health had become a priority due to the massive increase of Trench Foot.[56] Bert, his

---

[56] A painful condition of the feet caused by long immersion in cold water or mud and marked by blackening and death of surface tissue. Severe cases resulted in a soldier's removal from active duty until recovered.

35th Battalion and the 9th Brigade were moving out to the Ypres sector and the front line.

On strength, the 9th Brigade under the command of Lieutenant Colonel Goddard consisted of 34 officers, 89 non-commissioned officers and 867 soldiers.[57] The march to Ypres was 48 miles (78km). A daily breakdown of the journey organized by command, and billeting arrangements were made where possible to ensure safe and expedient transit. The sighting of planes became more frequent and often resulted in a scramble to roadside cover to avoid the bombs. Anticipation was on the rise as was Bert's silent laments. Bert's were of home. Blanche and his children were with him always.

The daily transit schedule set by Brigade Command was:[58]

Wednesday 26 September 1917, left Wismes on route to trenches. Marched via Lumbres and Wisernes and Blendecques to billets nest of Renescure. Owing to difficulties in finding billeting areas, first day's march was about 25 miles (40km). Halts every 15 minutes, midday halt 12-100pm. Arrive billets 6.00pm.

Thursday 27 September 1917, 6.00am resumed march to St. Sylvestre and Eeck 16 miles (26km) to the northwest. Arrived 2.00pm.

Friday 28 September 1917, march resumed 7.00am to Steenvoorde camp near Winnezeele. All settled in with billets at 1.00pm.

Saturday 29 September 1917, the 35th and 36th Battalions advance to Ypres 18 miles (30km) to mobilize in preparation to relieve 8th Infantry Brigade (English).

Sunday 30 September 1917, moved by motor buses to relieve the 13th King's Own regiment north of the Zonnebeke railway 5 miles (7km). 35th Battalion on the right, 36th Battalion on the left.

---

[57] War Diary Volume X 9th Australian Infantry Brigade, August 1917.
[58] War Diary of the 35th Battalion for the month of September 1917.

Bert's last days.

Bert and the 35th entered Ypres in formation under the command of Lieutenant Colonel Henry Goddard. It was evident that the bitter winter had set in. The mud and the cold made it almost unbearable. The battlefields were tracks of churned up soil, mud, equipment and horses. Men and beasts had drowned in a sea of slime and liquid mud. They were also confronted with movement and activity from every direction. Field ambulances, both motorized and horse driven, were transporting the wounded. Troops were either going to the front or coming from the front. The difference in appearance of both was contrasting. Bert noticed the dishevelled and exhausted appearance of those coming from the line. Very little organization or form in their stride, muddied from head to foot and an indifferent glaze, void of emotion, seemed to be predominant. There were stretcher bearers, four to a stretcher, depositing their loads to the field hospital 150 yards north of the ruins that were once Ypres Cathedral. A spectacular example of medieval architecture was now an almost indistinguishable pile of rubble as was the rest of the town. Flares lit the night sky complimented by the lingering orange glow of each exploding round of canon fire. "Hell was just over the hill", Bert thought to himself.

Ypres was badly knocked about. Even though Bert had more on his mind he pondered on the soaring ruin of the steeple and imagined what it may have been like just a few years earlier. Prior to the war, the town was a hive of industry containing factories of all descriptions. A testament to the industrial revolution, it was especially regarded for processing fabrics, cotton and canvas. Like most emerging provincial towns in France prior to the war, civilians would have carried on with their avocations, whilst cafes and other small enterprises would have reaped the benefits from a continual flow of merchants travelling through to Paris. Bert wondered if the petit Mesdemoiselles that came around to his billets in the cold dark hours of the wintery mornings with cakes and cups of hot coffee, for which they charged deux sous (two half pennies) provided the same service here. He doubted it. Young boys however, who soldiers called petit Garcons, were allowed as far as the subsidiary lines to sell to the troops the daily papers and other available assortments.

Soon after entering the town's centre, Bert and the troops were startled by a sudden bombardment. They did not know whether it was the howitzers or the planes delivering their loads. It was Bert's first real encounter with the enemy. It was during this shelling another one of the 35th's casualties occurred. A poor soul in the wrong place was killed by a bomb. He was a single casualty with men no further than 20 feet away, walking away without a scratch. Such as it was, Bert realized that luck was going to play a huge part in his survival in this dark and bloodied place. Word was that the dead soldier was one of the battalion's sergeants and was standing near the church close to the animal enclosure when hit.

In the early hours of the morning of Monday 1 October 1917, under the cover of darkness illuminated only by a dull moon and the occasional flare, Menere's 35th stole silently across Half-Past Eleven Square and Barbed-Wire Square, which were enveloped in a blanket frost. Not the clean sheen of white frost like that of the Grampians in August, but a composite of ice, manure, mud and occasionally flesh. They were loaded up with full packs and equipment and went steadily on until a large red building was reached. This was called 'The Gum-boot Store.' Here every man was issued with a pair of rubber boots which had to be returned when their rotation in the trenches was over. These boots reached from the toes up to the thighs, and after a while, created a freezing sensation in the feet. They seemed to accumulate as much moisture as they were designed to keep out. This was due to the condensing of the perspiration from the body. Alongside of the Gumboot Store was a Red Cross canteen where tea and biscuits could be obtained prior to entering the trenches. No matter how good the gum boots were, stinking trench foot was almost a certainty during the relentless wet winter of 1917.

The entrance to the system of trenches in front of Zonnebeke Railway was eventually achieved. The guides, on this night, did their job well. It was a communication trench called Lunatic Lane, so named after the Lunatic Asylum, which stood at the head.

It was tough going getting through the trenches with their full loads and an unauthorized blanket or two. This was a newbie's error because the troops exiting the trenches took possession, under orders, of the extra blankets. A lesson learnt; blankets and other possessions, not essential in the front trenches, were left at the quartermaster's store prior to taking over the line and they were retrieved when they too were eventually relieved.

The first night in the trenches, Monday 1 October 1917, was unexpectedly slow with intermittent shelling raids rather than a continual bombardment. A pleasing feature, and to Bert a welcome surprise, was to discover how well the organization of the battalion was being maintained. The transport brought their limbers right up close to the firing line. Working and carrying parties traversing forwards and backwards like streams of ants, kept the troops supplied with ammunition, wire and all the necessities for carrying on warfare. Forwards and backwards but still in range of an exploding shell or sniper's bullet, the liquidous mud in and out of the trenches made every task, every step, difficult.

The comfort of the men was not neglected. The battalion cooks, who were referred to as 'The Babbling Brooks', setup their travelling kitchens in the subsidiary lines.[59] There were four of these cookers, one to each company. Throughout the day the cooks kept each company supplied with hot food. There was tea, morning and evening, and stew at midday. These meals were brought up from the cooks by mess-orderlies who worked together in pairs. Strapped to the back of one of them was a large vacuum container filled with either stew or tea. These were always acceptable and generally quite hot.

The mess-orderlies also distributed the large army biscuits that could alleviate any hunger pang on account of their thickness and weight. They also distributed issues of cheese, tins of bully beef, jam and bread. The latter, when plentiful, would work out at a daily ration of 'four men to a loaf.' These commodities were carried around in sandbags, which had a way of shedding their jute hairs on the contents, especially on the cheese and margarine which was the name of the substitute for butter.

How different the trenches were to what Bert thought they would be. His vision was that you got on the fire step and shot a Hun any old time, providing that he didn't get you in the meantime. What really happens is this; You keep your head below the parapet and if by chance you get curious as to what is happening on the other side, you do so with the aid of periscope or

---

[59] Situated (usually) 2 lines behind the front line.

51

risk increasing a Hun sniper's kill tally. And as for seeing a Hun – well a few of the boys in the 35th found out right early which end of a Hun is harmful. Fritz was keen on the sniping, and they were good. During the early part of the game, they had the better of the 35th but the Aussie boys soon figured it out and became a genuine problem for any German keen enough to do a loo run or be in the open at the wrong time.

The Hun's most effective weapon of attack was the Minenwerfer. A species of trench mortar that hurls a cask of high explosives (H.E.) about the size and shape of a demijohn.[60] One can see them coming but that avails little as they are like a cross-eyed person: they never go where they are looking. Particularly offensive. Next comes the whizz-bang. A thing like a red devil that comes too straight and quick to be termed a mortar. It cannot be dodged. By the time its heard, the Whizz has knocked the head of someone half a mile behind you and some seconds later you hear the bang.[61]

In the early hours of Tuesday 2 October 1917, Bert and the 35th were moved through the mud and slime of the trenches to secure the right side of the railway approximately 150 yards from the station. Much happened that night with continuous bombing and gas alerts. Very little ground was gained, and every effort was made, particularly by Bert, not to raise his head. They were pinned down by constant bombardment. It seemed to Bert that the noise and the shock waves alone sucked the courage (and the ability to stand-up) from his very soul. Through the surrounding haze of lyddite,[62] fog and dust Bert could see that he was not the only one questioning his ability and willingness to do the job. The German artillery had pinpointed their positions amongst the constant illumination from the flares. The brigade's advance was not letting up and the orders clear. Bert was scared and convinced that the next shell burst would take with it his last breath. None-the-less Archi Campbell, Andy Parker, Rudi Ford and Bert Menere were organized to retrieve the fallen resulting from this latest push. They did their job as stretcher bearers.

---

[60] A large, narrow-necked glass or earthenware typically used to transport liquids.
[61] Extracted from the diary of Chas Harris. B (and D) Coy. 19/3/1917. Sourced http://www.firstaif.info/diaries/hell_babes.htm.
[62] A high explosive containing picric acid, used chiefly by the British during WW1.

The night sky continued to be illuminated by flares and occasionally yellow chlorine-based gas. Gas masks were required. The masks would fog up and seeing was difficult. Peripheral vision impossible. If the mask was removed to get a better look, the gas would immediately hit the eyes and back on went the mask. The effects of gas were horrible. A German invention, they knew how to use it for maximum effect.[63] It was an impossible night and ultimately, the fifty yards gained were relinquished by early morning. Nonetheless, a path had been laid to enable the AIF's 3rd Division to strike at the main Broodseinde Ridge – the last obstacle between the allies and Fritz's defensive Hindenburg Line. This was going to be a big offensive and the 35th was gearing up to commence at dawn on Thursday October 4, 1917. *"For the first time, the two ANZAC Corps – four Divisions would be side by side…. To summarize, twelve divisions and parts of two others would attack on a 14000 yards' front."*[64]

The 35th Battalion, along with 60,000 other ANZAC troops, were now mobilizing to be part of this historic push. The Anzac engineers and pioneers had spent the two previous days laying duckboards along the tracks to cater for the march forward to the front lines. Because of uncertain weather and lack of time, this task was not completed which would inevitably hinder the mobilization of all brigades. Once again, the mud, slush and slime of the Belgium winter of 1917 was an added burden to all advancing troops.

Albert Menere would not be part of the Broodseinde battle launching on 4 October, nor the Passchendaele offensive that was to take place within the following days and weeks. On the morning of Thursday 2 October 1917, Bert's life ended. His wife Blanche and her six young children had lost the man who led their family. His active part on the front lines in the 'war to end all wars', lasted only three days and nights. He was a stretcher bearer on the bloodiest battlefield in history. His final moments were in a low-lying trench located 150 yards north of the parapet adjacent to the Zonnebeke

---

[63] "Had the Germans known what a powerful weapon they had in gas, they would have reached Paris, because they had killed 2000 men and captured 60 guns the first time they used it." Lieutenant McDonald, 21st Infantry Battalion. Sourced: An Anzacs War Diary, Ed. A.D.Bell, p 33.
[64] CEW Bean, Official History of Australia in War 1914-18, Angus and Robertson, Sydney, 1933, p837.

Railway Station. He was with four other stretcher bearers.[65] Private H Bradley (No. 1871, 35th Battalion) was near the explosion and survived the blast. His words recounting the event,

> "*We were holding the line in the early morning. I was very close to Ford and Menere when the shell dropped near them killing them both instantly. They were badly knocked about; I saw them buried just over the parapet where they fell in the open. Their graves were marked by a rough cross with their names. They were buried in separate graves. There would be very little chance of finding the place the ground had been knocked about so much[66]. Pte Parker of the 35th Battalion was killed at the same time and buried at the same place.*"[67]

Lieutenant Colonel Henry Arthur Goddard – From his diary on entering Ypres Saturday 29 September 1917. Titled '*Tour of a Company in the Front Line*'.[68]

Lieutenant Colonel Henry Arthur Goddard was commander of the 35th Battalion. The following is his first-hand account of the movements of the 35th as he and his battalion entered the Ypres sector on the Saturday 29 September 1917. Albert Henri Menere marched in with this contingent and his death noted in this account.

> "*It was on the 29th of September 1917 that we marched through the ruins of historic YPRES. The night was dull and cloudy and obscured the young moon, the roads were congested with heavy traffic, ammunition and ration limbers[69], an occasional field gun or howitzer, together with moving troops made frequent stops a necessity. Overhead, the Hun planes were dropping bombs on the*

---

[65] The others killed were stretcher bearers according to eyewitness statement of R.G.Drew (7243) taken from No.4 Australian General Hospital, Randwick, 14.10.18.
[66] The inability to locate graves meant that Menere, Parker and Ford would be forever part on the Menin Gate Memorial for the 40,000 allied soldiers killed with no remains to be formally buried.
[67] This quote sourced from Australian Red Cross Wounded and Missing Enquiry Bureau Files. Statement dated 7 March 1917, Havre, France. The statement was a part of Bradley's account of Ford's death which gave mention to Menere, and others killed.
[68] AWM., Papers relating to the narrative history of the 35th Battalion compiled by Henry Arthur Goddard.
[69] Ration Limber is like a horse drawn dray.

numerous camps and horse lines. As the battalion moved through YPRES along the MENEIN ROAD a bomb was dropped in the middle of the street, resulting in casualties to some outgoing British troops and just missed a platoon of our Australian lads.

Our Battalion had not previously been in this sector, and everything seemed strange. The gaunt misshapen shell torn buildings looked ghastly in the dim light. As we passed the famous Cloth Hall, we peered through the shadows to try and form some idea of its pre-war beauty, but the Hun shells had so torn it that little of the original structure remained. It was only in later days that we were able to examine it more closely. It made us feel that war with a big W was in progress and it meant work with a bigger W before the job of knocking out the Hun would be complete. We passed over the famous ramparts which must have taken years to build and crossed the old moat which formed a serious obstacle to attackers in days gone by. We rested here for a few minutes and then swung out along the road on our way to ZONNEBEKE. Many heavily freighted motor ambulances passed us and the occasional stretcher bearer borne by 4 men taking their burden to the nearest dressing station in the town. We passed that well known spot Hell Fire Corner, nor did we linger in passing. It was very noticeable how the drivers of the mule teams as they neared this spot whipped up their mounts and cleared it at breakneck speed. The country, or as much of it as we could see in the pale moon light, the sky by this time partially cleared, presented a miserable spectacle. What trees remained were blasted and the debris of overturned wagons and other vehicles as well as the few battered houses were sufficient evidence of what had occurred throughout the whole length of this road.

About a mile from Hell Fire Corner, we rested. While sitting on our packs a Fritz bombing plane passed over. It was quite visible against the fleecy white clouds which partially obscured the moon. A machine gun within a few yards of us opened fire and it was interesting to watch the tracer bullets speeding towards the plane, but apparently no damage was done as it continued its course towards the town. Shells were bursting with greater frequency near the road than had been the case up till that time. After the plane had passed the lads lit their fags and as usual started all sorts of discussions. One I remember well as it made me laugh heartily at the time. The subject was not a new one and it referred to chats. "Well, Bill, I've never had a single bloody Chat[70] on me". "Neither have I" replied Bill, "all my bloody chats are married and have bloody big families".

We made another start and after marching about twenty minutes we met our guides, members of the .... Regt. These led us by platoons along the road past Breman House, a large concrete pillbox, captured from the Huns to the YPRES-ROULERS railway crossing at which point we left the road and moved along a track at the side of the railway embankment. Mud, mud, mud we sank over our boot tops, then our knees, and being heavily laden with packs etc. our progress was sadly impeded. Enemy machine gun occasionally opened fire and the hiss over our heads, like bees in flight, was not particularly reassuring. The air was tainted by the disgusting smell of decomposing human flesh and dead men were here frequently in evidence. Fortunately, we had not much further to go. We were led by our guides into so-called trenches. What little information as to the position of the enemy, machine guns, etc., was obtained from the outgoing Company Commander and we were left to place our men to what we considered the best advantage. Trench stores, there were none, unless one bottle of soda water can be considered as war material.

The Battalion was split into two companies, one company to the front and one in support about 50 yards to the rear. My company "B" was on the left, "A" was on the right with its right flank on the ROULERS Railway line, a hundred yards or so on the YPRES side of the ruined village of ZONNEBEKE. The 36th Battalion was on our left. Each company front was about 400 yards. The line was evidently a new one as the trenches

---

[70] A 'chat' according to old Australian slang is a derogatory term for an unattractive female.

were very poor, being shallow, undrained and badly sighted. The conditions were about as miserable as can be imagined. No wire had been erected in front and no dugouts or shelters of any kind existed. Company Headquarters of "B" company was a shell hole about 5 yards behind the front line and towards morning a drizzling rain commenced to fall, the discomfort of our conditions was greatly increased. The early dawn showed the enemy lines on Hill 40 from 100 to 150 yards in front. A concrete pillbox in their front line was opposite the centre of our sector.

As the light increased it was evident from the frequent sniping that the Hun was not going to allow us to show ourselves, with impunity. Good spots were chosen for our snipers, and it was not long before they made Fritz very careful about exposing himself. Good sport was always obtained by picking men off as they attempted to enter or leave the pill box. For some reason they had to expose themselves at this point. The first day our snipers had so improved matters that we could occasionally look over the top without being certain of having a bullet whistling within a few inches of our heads. The British troops holding this portion of the line had evidently made an attack some days previously and had fallen back to the line held by us as many dead were lying both in front and to the rear of our trenches and the decomposing bodies were making the air very foul. It was therefore necessary to arrange during the next night for burial parties to inter all the bodies within reasonable distance forward of the front line, and between the front and support lines. This entailed quite a lot of work and during the day and at night all men available were employed improving the trenches and connecting isolated positions so that supervision could be more easily maintained. The enemy shelling of this position of the line was intermittent and except on rare occasions, not violent. The night following that on which the trenches were taken over, the enemy dropped some heavy shell rounds about the front line. One 5.9 fell in the front line immediately opposite *company headquarters and unfortunately a party was working in the bay at the time. Three men were killed[71] and five were wounded. In order to instance how one must become accustomed to the disgusting sights of the battlefield I would mention that the company orderly room Corporal who was in the front line for the first time was sent by the Company Commander to assist the evacuation of the wounded and disposal of the dead. On his return from this unpleasant work with his hands and clothes smeared with blood he remarked "If anyone had told me that I could collect the entrails and limbs of men and put them in sandbags without fainting or breaking down I would have said it was impossible".[72]*

---

[71] The three men killed were Albert Henri Menere (7283), Andrew Parker (2023), Rudolf Sydney Ford (1902A). One of the 5 wounded was most likely George Salter.
[72] Thus ends Lieutenant Colonel Henry Arthur Goddard's personal account of the 35th's Battalion's march to the Ypres-Zonnebeke up to the night of 2nd September and the final stage of A.H.Menere's life as a soldier, husband, father.

Chapter 12

Mrs Menere, it is with deep regret that...

My husband, my life,
You left us alone.
We were afraid and scared for you,
So far from our home.

The days you were gone,
Were filled with hope and dread.
'til finally it happened,
We heard you were dead!

'Why did you go?' by Brandt, 2025

World War 1, particularly during 1917, was the catalyst that ignited women's rights in Australia. When Australia sent her young men to the battle fields of Europe, there were fewer able-bodied Australians to fulfil what were traditionally male vocations. Blanch was one of the many women left on the home front to cope with a different set of challenges. Some women stepped up to contribute to the war effort by working munitions, agriculture, and other trade-based jobs usually reserved for men. Blanche had six young children all under the age of ten, to care for, alone. In 1917 the eldest was Aubrey (10 years), followed by Raymond (9 years), Aureole (5 years), Edward (4 years), Albert (3 years), and Leila 2 (years). Blanche's and Bert's extended families were in Victoria and not very helpful in providing any physical support.

Alone in an increasingly depressed societal mood, Blanche had to deal with ever increasing prices for food and groceries.[73] She had to keep her young family together. At 33 years of age, she was always tired. The three eldest children attended school 800 metres away at St Peter's Public School. The rest were at home. A small backyard at 56 King Street gave them some room to play and be children. Bert's four fifths allocation of his pay to Blanche equated to 8 shillings per day. This complimented the food stamps that were the real currency in 1917 for the working and middle classes. Blanche and her children were never hungry, but it was tough.

St Peter's Catholic Church at Surrey Hills was twenty minutes' walk for Blanche and her kids. This was her Sunday salvation and during the week provided some respite from the darkness of worrying. The wives and mothers of those abroad would meet during the week and provide support for each other. All too often they were called upon to support the grieving when notification of 'Missing in Action' or 'Killed in Action' (K.I.A.) was received. Confirmed K.I.A.s were published in the Sydney Morning Herald or local papers. By the time publication of the fallen had been issued, families had been notified well beforehand of their loved one's passing. The process of notification was usually a telegram 2-6 weeks after the event. Sometimes a 'Missing in Action' would precede a confirmed K.I.A. A soldier's death needed to be confirmed by eyewitnesses and then further collaborated by army hierarchy. This could delay the process by months, especially if a soldier's body was not recovered from the battlefield.

As the months rolled on letters from Bert became sporadic. Mail was delayed due to enemy naval actions in and about the English Channel and the Atlantic ports. She did, however, receive a beautiful embroided cushion cover. This arrived late November. An accolade of love beside the AIF Coat of Arms together with a studio portrait of Albert provided a tangible connection for Blanche to hold onto. It made Blanche feel good. Blanche did send care packages abroad. These were put together in collaboration with her church friends and the support group. She wondered if Bert received them.

---

[73] The price of food and groceries had increased by 30% over the previous 3 years.

On the home front anxiety levels, especially amongst the women, were high. Politics was always in the newspapers and on the radio and were a prominent part of the conversations at Blanche's church group's get togethers. Blanche shared the anxiety. Conscription was a divisive issue especially when a second referendum was defeated in 1917.[74] Blanche was undecided about the issue of conscription. So many losses with no end in sight to the war. What was the point in sending more young Australians to an uncertain future? Only now, in 1917, was a close-to-accurate account of early battles, such as Frommels, being released to the Australian public. The real devastation of the war on our Australian soldiers was starting to emerge. The workers' strikes[75] on the eastern seaboard lead by high-profile women got Blanche's attention. She admired the likes of Adela Pankhurst[76] standing up for those on the Homefront. Like Adela, Blanche felt the terrible grief and experienced the consequences that so many other Australian families were enduring during 1917.

When bad news had to be dispensed, the army did its best to hand deliver the telegrams or organize parish priests or their representatives to complete the task. How terrible it would have been to receive the 'pink telegram of death'[77] delivered by the postman? Blanche dreaded any knock on her door and then one day, it happened. The telegram Blanche received indicated 'Killed in Action'. The circumstances of Albert's death would not be officially confirmed until the due process undertaken by the 'Australian Red Cross Society Wounded and Missing Enquiry Bureau'[78] was completed. This reached Blanche in late March 1918.

---

[74] There were 2 referendums, 1916 and 1917, set by Prime Minister Billy Hughes. Both were defeated.
[75] Strike involved an estimated 97,000 workers and to place primarily in Melbourne. Rioting and damage to properties especially along the docks accompanied these strikes and was a true reflection of the shifting mood in Australia during 1917.
[76] Adela Constantia Mary Walsh (nee) Pankhurst; 19 June 1885 – 23 May 1961) was a Britishborn suffragette who worked as a political organizer for the Women's Political and Social Union (WSPU) in Scotland. In 1914 she moved to Australia where she continued her activism and was co-founder of both the Communist Party of Australia and the Australia First Movement.
[77] 'The Pink telegram' was used to inform the immediate family of the death of their family member. The term became symbolic of bad news during the war period.
[78] The Australian Red Cross Wounded and Missing Enquiry Bureau was established in 1915 to assist families in locating missing, wounded, and captured soldiers during World War I. The bureau, often staffed by volunteers, relied on official lists and interviews with comrades to investigate inquiries from families.

Blanche was busy at home on Friday 12 November 1917[79] when she heard the knock on her front door. Like hundreds of wives and mothers before and after her, Blanche's heart missed a beat when she saw Father Collender, the parish priest from St Peter's, Surry Hills on her doorstep. She tried to usher Aureole and Leila, who were by her side, into the lounge room and away from the news Blanche knew was coming. It didn't work, they sensed something was wrong.

Father Collender had been allocated the task of informing her that her husband, Private Albert Henri Menere, AIF 3rd Division, 9th Infantry Brigade, 35th Battalion, was killed in action on the Belgium front on Tuesday 2 October 1917. The dreaded 'Pink telegram'[80] was in Father Collender's left hand as he entered the residence of the remaining Meneres.

It read:

> COMMONWEALTH OF AUSTRALIA Form No 144
> Postmaster-General's Department, New South Wales
> URGENT TELEGRAM
> This Message has been received subject to the Post and Telegraph Act and Regulations. All Complaints to be addressed in writing to the Deputy Postmaster-General
>
> Station From, No. of Words, and Check
> Victoria Barracks 69 5/5 12 40 RP section 9 5 Rev Elwin Manly
>
> Br 213 Officially reported that Number (Br 213) (7283 Pte A.H.Menere) 35th Battalion previously reported missing now killed in action 2nd October 1917. Please inform Mother (Mrs B.E.A. Menere 56 King Street Newtown) and convey deep regret and sympathy of their Majesties the King and Queen and the Commonwealth Government in loss that she and Army have sustained by death soldier reply paid Col Luscombe 1 5H
>
> Date stamp and received 1st November 1917

---

[79] An estimated date based on the timeline of her war pension approval.
[80] This telegram formatted from an original 'Pink Telegram' from 1917.

Albert had been away for only nine months, but he and his wife had corresponded regularly. She had sent him a comfort parcel. Albert and his mates made short work of it on the train journey to one of the training camps. Albert had sent Blanche a fine tapestry with a photograph amongst other things. It was inevitable with the large number of casualties in World War I that many wives and mothers received letters or parcels from their husbands or sons fighting in Europe after being told of their deaths. And so, it was with Blanche Menere. The cushion cover commissioned by Bert in Etables early in September was not received by Blanche until after he had fallen.

Blanche and her six young children were grief stricken. The uncertainty of a future in such tumultuous times hung heavily on the shoulders of the newly widowed young mother. Her friends from her church did their best to support Blanche through her darkest of times.

Chapter 13

A grave lost, a name on a wall.

"HALT! Thy tread is on heroes' graves;
Australian lads lie sleeping below;
Just rough wooded crosses at their heads,
To let their comrades know."

Extract from 'Fallen Comrades, (A voice from Gallipoli)'.
Skeyhill, p.33

Albert Henri Menere's body was buried on the night he was killed. He was buried where he fell, 150 yards (137m) to the left of the parapet adjacent to the Zonnebeke railway station. He was buried with the other soldiers killed by the same explosion. Due to the incessant shelling, they were unburied and then buried again. Within days the rain, sludge and chaos of the bloody battlefield engulfed the burial sites, and the graves were no more. Albert Menere was one of 724 Allied soldiers killed on that day and his would be one of the 54,389 names inscribed on the Menin Gate Memorial Wall (Bay 25), representing those dead who could not be identified or were not recovered from the battlefield. Part of the confirmation of death process was to compile eyewitness accounts of the incident. The following are accounts of those who were witness to Bert's death and provide an integral part of this research. They exist in original hand-written form and were collated and transcribed by the Australian Red Cross Society Wounded and Missing Enquiry Bureau files.

356 Leslie John Avery.[81]

Left of Railway cutting Ypres, Zonnebeke. Killed by a shell, I saw Private: 7283 Albert Henri MENERE'S body but I don't know where buried. Pay Corporal 3524A THOMAS JOHN JORDON CLARKE was in charge of burying at the time.

Ward 39 Harefield, England.
6th February 1918.

3524A Thomas John Jordon Clarke.[82]

(Pay Corporal) 35th Battalion AIF. Re: Private: 7283 Albert Henri MENERE. "I have to inform you that he was Killed in Action on the night of October 1st 1917. He was on duty as a stretcher bearer in front line when he was killed by H.E shell which burst in trench at 8.15 p.m. killing him instantly and to bring his body out was almost impossible owing to the trench communication. I buried him alongside two comrades in a shell hole just south of Zonnebeke Railway Station and erected a small wooden cross to mark the spot. His pocket wallet etc, were sent on through to the Regimental Chaplain to Base. Private MENERE was held in high esteem by all who knew him. Though he was not long with this unit, yet he soon won the admiration of his comrades by his cheerful disposition. On the night he was killed just previously to the occurrence I was talking to him, and he was in high spirits. Private MENERE was of short build, dark complexion and rather stout.

London.
12th February 1918.

---

[81] Australian Red Cross Society Wounded and Missing Enquiry Bureau files.
[82] Australian Red Cross Society Wounded and Missing Enquiry Bureau files, 1914-18 War IDRL/0428.

7221 John Ernest Canham.[83]

35th Battalion AIF. B Company No: 5 Platoon. I know that Private: 7720 William Archibald CAMPBELL 35th Battalion AIF. B Company No: 5 Platoon was with Private: 7283 Albert Henri MENERE when he (Menere) was killed. They were both stretcher bearers and CAMPBELL could give you full information. MENERE came with the 24th Reinforcements. He was a very thick set man, about 5ft 8" slightly grey in B VI. He came from Melbourne and was an engineer of some sort.

No:2 Australian General Hospital
Boulogne, France.
7th March 1918.

1871A Henry Bradley.[84]

B Company No: 6 Platoon. 35th Battalion AIF. "I knew Private: 1902A Rudolph Sydney FORD very well. He was in B Company No: 5 Platoon and came from Junction Point via Crookwell, New South Wales. He was a farm Labourer. I Knew Private: 7283 Albert Henri MENERE slightly. He was in B Company No: 5 or 6 Platoon. On the 2nd of October we were at Zonnekebe. We were holding the line in the early morning. I was very close to FORD and MENERE when a shell dropped near them, killing them both instantly. They were badly knocked about.

I saw them buried just over the parapet where they fell in the open. Their graves were marked with a rough cross with their names. They were buried in separate graves. There would be very little chance of finding the place the ground has been knocked about so much. Private: 2023 Andrew William PARKER of the 35th Battalion B Company 6th Platoon (not listed) was killed at the same

---

[83] Australian Red Cross Society Wounded and Missing Enquiry Bureau files, 1914-18 War IDRL/0428.
[84] Australian Red Cross Society Wounded and Missing Enquiry Bureau files, 1914-18 War IDRL/0428.

time and buried at the same place, and also Private: 1453 George SALTER of the 35th Battalion B Company 7th Platoon (not on the list) was wounded by the same shell, and died on his way down to the Dressing Station."

Harve Hospital, France.
15th March 1918.
(Author's Note: Private: 1453A George SALTER was Wounded in Action on the 12th of October 1917 and returned to Australia on the 9th of December 1919.)

7228 William Archibald Campbell.[85]

35th Battalion AIF B Company No: 5 Platoon. Re Private: 7283 Albert Henri MENERE'S death. The only information I can give you is that he was a comrade of mine ever since leaving Australia and I was close by him when he was killed by a shell and we buried him at night on the battlefield, but to tell you the exact place I can't. He might be numbered but I will ask our Chaplain when I see him and if he knows anymore, I will write and let you know, but you can take my word it is correct as I was alongside him when he was killed. I was going to write to his people, but I did not know their address, but he wasn't buried in a cemetery as it was a pretty hot place. I also have his photo here now if it would be of use to you for identification you can let me know and I will send it to you at the shortest notice.

London.
14th October 1918.

7234 Robert George Drew.[86]

35th Battalion AIF. "We were holding the front-line trenches at Zonnebeke. Private: 7283 Albert Henri

---

[85] Australian Red Cross Society Wounded and Missing Enquiry Bureau files.
[86] Australian Red Cross Society Wounded and Missing Enquiry Bureau files.

MENERE and three other stretcher bearers were sitting on the side of a trench when a shell fell among them. A piece hit MENERE and killed him at once. He was buried where he was hit.

No: 4 Australian General Hospital.
Randwick, New South Wales.

Chapter 14

The 35ᵗʰ Battalion marches on.

Keep on pushing lads,
The Hun's on the run.
He's tired of fighting,
He's almost done.

It's been a tough fight,
And we did our best,
To make things right,
Before we rest.

'Almost there Boys', by Brandt, 2025

During that first week of October 1917 in which Albert Menere was killed, the soldiers of the 35ᵗʰ Battalion served in the Battle of Broodseinde. Heavy rain had deluged the battlefield and thick mud tugged at the advancing troops and fouled their weapons. The battle was a disaster for the 35ᵗʰ; 508 men crossed the start line but only 90 remained unwounded at the end.[87] In the period 13 July – 12 October 1917, the British and Her Commonwealth Forces had accumulated casualties of 448,614 compared with 217,700 for the Germans.[88]

Between 20 September and 4 of October 1917, the British and Australian forces, the 35ᵗʰ included, had struck three major blows against the Germans, the last being the Battle of Broodseinde. This battle alone caused German General Erich Ludendorff to refer to the battle as, "The Black day of the 4ᵗʰ

---

[87] Source www.diggerhistory.info.
[88] Source www.diggerhistory.info.

of October."[89] This battle played an important part in turning the tide of the war against Germany. Ludendorff also stated, "The battle was extraordinarily severe, and again we only came though it with enormous losses". Furthermore, German General von Kuhl stated via an official monograph "No battle in the war could compare in dreadfulness, this battle (Broodseinde) was the worst of the war, so bloody."[90]

The 35th Battalion's participation in the battles of Polygon Wood, Broodseinde and Passchendaele cost over half a million lives in its three months duration. The Germans lost about 250,000 lives and the British 300,000 of whom 36,500 were Australian. Over 90,000 British and Australian bodies were never identified, 42,000 were never recovered. These had been blown into pieces or had drowned and been consumed in the dreadful morass. Many of the drowned were exhausted or wounded men who had slipped or fallen off the duckboards and were unable to escape the filthy, foul-smelling glutinous mud, sinking deeper to their deaths as they struggled.

The battles of Polygon Wood, Broodseinde and Passchendaele also epitomized the extraordinary commitment of the ANZAC and his fighting soldier brothers. According to historical accounts, the plan was regarded as improbable in victory. Field Marshal Douglas Haig convinced his parliament of a victory and as history has recorded, he was correct. In late 1917, the Passchendaele offensive set the scene for the allies' final offensive against the German Spring Offensive of 1918.

As part of the Spring Offensive, the 35th Battalion was deployed to defend the lines in Amiens and Villers-Bretonneux. The battalion took part in an offensive attack at Hangard Wood on 30 March 1918, and helped to defeat a major enemy push at Villers-Bretonneux on 4 April 1917. It was becoming evident to British Command that despite early gains, the German's Spring Offensive was failing. The Allied Forces' relentless progression and the Hun's diminishing supplies were contributing factors. Haig's declaration of an 'All Arms Strategy' that combined infantry, artillery, tank and air power, proved to be a deciding factor in

---

[89] Eric Ludendorff, Britannica.com.
[90] Hermann von Kuhl, en.wikiquotes.org.

overcoming the last defence line held by the Germans. The stage was set for the Allies' final victory and on 8 August 1918, the Allies launched what was to be their final big push, the 'Hundred Days Offensive.'[91] The 35th was again committed to the fighting.

Following the Hundred Days Offensive, much of the Australian Corps were removed from the line for rest.[92] The 35th Battalion had been severely depleted and were suffering from acute manpower shortages. This reflected most A.I.F Battalions. The shortage was a due to a combination of a decrease in the number of volunteers from Australia, and the decision to grant home leave to men who had served for over four years.[93] November 11th, 1918, heralded the end of hostilities thus demobilization began and the men of the 35th Battalion were slowly repatriated back to Australia. Finally, in March 1919, the 35th Battalion was disbanded.[94] During the war, the 35th Battalion lost 581 men killed or died on active service, while a further 1,637 were wounded.[95] The collateral damage on the home front could not be measured with numbers and statistics. The families and children left behind had to deal with the consequences. Albert and Blanche Menere's story typified that of the many thousands of families left behind.

---

[91] 'Hundred Days Offensive' was not s specific Allied campaign, but rather the rapid series of Allied offensives that resulted in the final WW1 victory.
[92] Gray, p.108.
[93] Gray, p.109.
[94] AWM., First World War, 1914–1918 units, retrieved 16 October 2024.
[95] AWM., First World War, 1914–1918 units, retrieved 16 October 2024.

Chapter 15

After the War.

Down the gangplank, to the town that I love,
I left you four years ago, for France and the mud.

Finally, I'm home, but it doesn't feel right,
My backpack is empty, but it doesn't feel light.

The dead, the maimed, the men that I have killed,
These are the burdens, that I carry still.

'Unwanted Baggage', by Brandt, 2025

Hugh Lowe, who enlisted at the same time as Albert Menere and was his next-door neighbour at 58 King Street, St Peters, returned to Australia on 3rd September 1919. He served in the 2nd Field Bakery. There is no record of physical wounds. George Moore served in the 1st Battalion after being transferred from the 62nd Battalion. George never saw active service as he was sent back to Australia after being charged with escaping an army compound in England. He returned to Australia 17 December 1917, and it was noted on his discharge papers that the reason was 'overage'. He died in 1923 in Fremantle Hospital, Perth, W.A.

Arthur Henry Goddard was given command of the 9th Brigade late in 1918 with the rank of Brigadier General. After the Armistice he was awarded the Distinguished Service Order and the Belgium Croix de Guerre. He returned to Australia in 1920 to reside in Sydney and soon after resumed his importing business. He later became a commercial representative for the Times Australia. He died in Sydney on 24 October 1955.

On Friday November 23, 1917, the War Pension was officially applied for in support of Blanche Menere and her six children. It was granted under the War Pensions Act of 1914 – 1916. On 20 December 1917 the pension was issued: Two pounds per fortnight for Blanche, one pound per fortnight for Aubrey, 15 shillings per fortnight for Raymond and 10 shillings per fortnight for Aureole, Albert Henri (Junior), Edward and Leila.[96]

On Friday 13 September 1918, Blanche Menere signed for a consignment from the Defence Department, this being the personal effects of Albert Menere. The package contained 2 discs, photo, cards, silver matchbox and a French phrase book. The effects were dispatched from London on Tuesday 5 February 1918 and arrived in Melbourne on 7 September 1918.

A Memorial Scroll and Memorial Plaque (number 333524) were requested by Blanche Menere on 15 July 1922.[97] Authorisation for dispatch was given on 12 July 1922. Delivery was completed on 22 September 1922. Evidence suggests that the plaques, together with the medals were only issued after Blanche lodged a letter of request with the Officer in Charge of Base Records, dated 8 July 1922. Blanche indicated in the same correspondence of a change in address to 291 King Street (now the Princess Highway), Newtown. This could account for the delay in the issuing of the medals. Other addresses on Defence Record Files for Blanche Menere were:

12 Lowrie St, Newton, NSW, returned to sender from this address 29.7.21.
134 Wellington St, Waterloo, NSW, returned to sender from this address12.9.21.

It was not until Thursday 31 May 1923, that Bert's Victory Medals were issued and signed for by Blanche. The whereabouts of the medals are, to this day, unknown. They were not handed down to any of the Menere children. Evidence of this being a letter from Albert Menere (Jnr) dated 9 April 1963, to the Medals Section of the Victoria Barracks, Melbourne. This letter requested duplicates

---

[96] War Pensions Statement NSW No. 477 dated 26 November 1917.
[97] Receipted from Officer in Charge Base records, Victoria Barracks, Melbourne.

as the original medals were 'lost years ago and none of the family has any knowledge of their whereabouts'. Ultimately this request was denied as it was not policy at the time to reissue medals when the recipients were no longer alive.[98] It is interesting to note that Albert Menere (Jnr) signed this correspondence as ex. R.A.N. 1932-1946 o/n19575.

An additional letter of request dated 5 November 1943, was forwarded to War Records by Jack H. Menere[99] requesting information about his uncle Albert Henri Menere. Jack Menere was also seeking the date that his brother Douglas Menere was officially presumed dead. Further research indicates that Douglas Menere, Regimental No. 413876, served in the Australian Airforce during WW2. Jack Menere also signed his letter as ex-serviceman Cpl N.X.59268. It is an emerging fact that the Menere family's sacrifice and service to the protection of Australia extended well beyond the death of Albert Henri Snr in 1917.

William Ogg (13 March 1890 – 1966).

William Ogg was 24 years of age when the war broke out. Born in Scotland 13 March 1890 he resided in Sydney after migrating from Scotland. Research indicates he was a coal miner before immigrating. Further research revealed little about William Ogg's early days as an Australian resident except that he was occasionally a commercial salesman.

He married Blanche Menere in 1926, Blanche being 6 years older than him. Sometime before their marriage, or soon afterwards, Aureole (14 years), Albert (13 years), Edward (12 years), and Leila (10 years) were placed in a Catholic orphanage in the Corowa area of Victoria. It was stated by Aureole [100] to her daughter June[101] that William Ogg "Would not bring up another man's children."

---

[98] Correspondence 94-0101 6095 Dated 9th May 1963 from OIC Central Army Records Office. At this time A.H.Menere (Junior) lived at 142 Victoria St, West pennant Hills, NSW.
[99] The address of Jack H. Menere at this time was 55 Queen St, Campbelltown, NSW.
[100] The author's grandmother.
[101] The author's mother.

Selected Bibliography

Australian War Memorial, Canberra

AWM, Australian Imperial Force unit war diaries, 1914-18 war
Administrative staff, Headquarters, 3rd Australian Division
9th Infantry Brigade
35th Infantry Battalion War Diary
36th Infantry Battalion War Diary
Australian War Memorial, Nominal Roll
1st Battalion Roll of Honour

Australian Red Cross Society Wounded and Missing Enquiry Bureau Files, 1914-18 War IDRL/0428

7283 Private Albert Henri Menere
1902A Private Rudolph Sidney Ford

National Archives of Australia
Series B2455 Australian Imperial Force Personnel Dossiers, 1914-1920

7283 Albert Henri Menere
2980 Percy Mingo Dwyer
3410 Walter Moore
7273 Hugh Lowe
7285 George Moore
3524A J. Clarke
7234 R.G. Drew
356 Leslie John Avery
7221 John Earnest Canham
1871A Henry Bradley

7228 William Campbell
1453A George Salter
2358 V8081 Albert Lowerson

Online resources

Duncan H., Merchant Fleets vol.1, P&O, Orient and Blue Anchor Lines' Commonwealth Gazette' No. 61. Retrieved from www.aif. adfa.edu.au:8080/showPerson?key=LOWERSON/AD/2358.

"The Spirit of the Forty-Second, Chapter 2", www.firstaif.info?42/ spirit/c2-adventure.htm   www.diggerhistory.info/pages-conflicts-periods/ww1/salisbury.htm.

Bayldon, Arthur, 'Institute of Australian Culture, Poetry 1901-53', https://www.australianculture.org/poetry-2.

Gilmore M., 'War – War Poetry, An Analysis', https://mous3ystar. weebly.com/war---mary-gilmore.html.

'Poetry Explorer, Your Free Poetry Website', https://www.poetry explorer.net

Unofficial History of the Australian and New Zealand Armed Services', http://www.diggerhistory.info.

Kuhl, Hermann von, 'Wikiquote', https://en.wikiquote.org/w/ index.php?search=kuhl&title=Special%3ASearch&ns0=1.

Ludendorff, Eric, 'Britannica', [https://www.britannica.com/biography/ Erich-Ludendorff.

Harris, C., 'Diary of Chas Harris (B and D) coy. 19/3/1917', http://www.firstaif/diaries/hell_babes.htm.

Bean, Charles, 'Australian Government Department of veteran Affairs, ANZAC Portal, The Newspaper men', https://anzacportal. dva.gov.au/wars-and-missions/ww1/personnel/anzac-legend#2.

Department of Veterans' Affairs, (2025), *William Dunstan*, DVA Anzac Portal, accessed 22 May 2025, https://anzacportal.dva.gov.au/stories/biographies/william-dunstan.

Published resources

Adam-Smith, P. '*The ANZACS*', Penguin

Bean, C. E. W. (1933). Official History of Australia in War 1914-1918. Angus and Robertson.

Clark, Margaret A. (2010). *Postcards from the Front, Still Going Strong*, Manning Valley Historical Society publishers.

Gray, R. (1991). *Kaiserschlacht, 1918: The Final German Offensive*. Osprey Campaign Series 11.

Harkins, J. M. (1919). *Idle Moments in the Line: A few Memories, in Plain Verse, of Life, Whilst on Active Service*. Moorabbin News.

James, N. D. G. (1987). *Plain Soldiering – A History of the Armed Forces on Salisbury Plain*. Hobnob.

Kearney, R. (2005). *Silent Voices: The story of the 10th Battalion AIF in Australia, Egypt, Gallipoli, France and Belgium during The Great War 1914-1918* (Chapter 19).

Lindsay, P. (2003). *The Spirit of the Digger: Then and Now*. Macmillan.

Rance, A. (1986). *Southampton, an illustrated history*. Milestone.

Returned Soldiers. (1918). *Diggers' Poems, Including the Landing at Gabe Tepe*, Timaru Post Print.

Ross, J. (Editor). (1990). *Chronicle of the 20th Century*. Chronicle.

Skeyhill, T. (1918). *Soldier Songs from ANZAC, Written in the Firing Line*, George Robertson and Company, Sydney.

The Australian Imperial Force in France, 1917 (11th edition). (1941).

Newspaper

The Weekend Australian, The Great War, Part Two: The Western Front, July 23-24, 2016.

The Weekend Australian, The Great War, Part Three: The Darkest Days, July 29-30, 2017.

Appendix

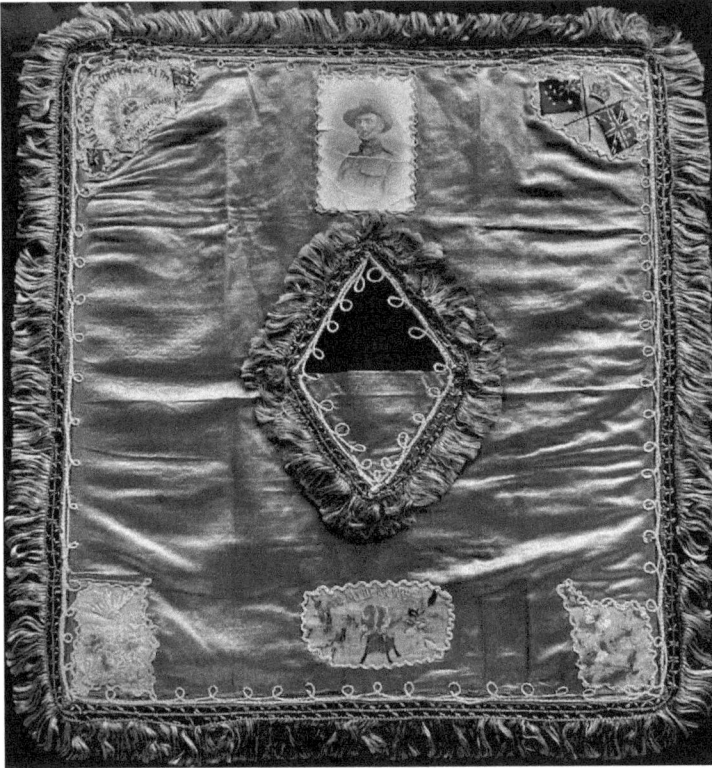

Appendix 1
Cushion cover with photograph of
Albert Menere

.